IN PRAISE OF
INTRANSIGENCE

IN PRAISE OF INTRANSIGENCE

The Perils of Flexibility

Richard H. Weisberg

OXFORD
UNIVERSITY PRESS

Oxford University Press is a department of the
University of Oxford. It furthers the University's objective
of excellence in research, scholarship, and education
by publishing worldwide.

Oxford   New York

Auckland   Cape Town   Dar es Salaam   Hong Kong   Karachi
Kuala Lumpur   Madrid   Melbourne   Mexico City   Nairobi
New Delhi   Shanghai   Taipei   Toronto

With offices in

Argentina   Austria   Brazil   Chile   Czech Republic   France   Greece
Guatemala   Hungary   Italy   Japan   Poland   Portugal   Singapore
South Korea   Switzerland   Thailand   Turkey   Ukraine   Vietnam

Oxford is a registered trade mark of Oxford University Press
in the UK and certain other countries.

Published in the United States of America by
Oxford University Press
198 Madison Avenue, New York, NY 10016

© Oxford University Press 2014

Library of Congress Cataloging-in-Publication Data
has been applied for.
ISBN 978-0-19-933498-8 (hardback)

9 8 7 6 5 4 3 2 1

Printed in the United States of America
on acid-free paper

TO THE SOUND INTERPRETERS:

Dan and Sara, Benno and Rachel, Sam and Adina,

and to the youngest among them,

Owen and Wes, and to my beloved Cheryl

Contents

Preface

Too often throughout history, crises have led people away from their own mature judgments about how to behave. In the face of the "new," individuals and institutions betray, sometimes quite quickly, their soundest traditions. Real or imagined "emergencies" provoke a flexible renegotiation of norms that had been in place for long periods and seemed both workable and good. Equivocating and distorting the best of their own beliefs, people act in ways that ultimately prove unwise and sometimes tragic. Only when the smoke clears do they recognize their folly. They return, too late for many who have been harmed by their flexibility, to their prior baseline practice.

I define "flexibility" here as a constant willingness, in the face of the inevitable newness of situations, to compromise even deeply held prior positions. I take "intransigence" to mean a resistance to the urge to shift malleably from traditions thought to be sound. Neither position brings with it any substantive conclusion about right and wrong; as I discuss, many intransigent positions are terribly misguided. The inquiry is not on the merits of any position but on a willingness to stick to it.

Just as there is no unity of judgment among the flexible, so there is rarely agreement on issues or beliefs among the intransigent, who are often wrongly lumped together as though they were a monolithic force for malevolence. Neither stance guarantees, for example, nonviolent as opposed to violent outcomes. Flexibility can bring on disastrous human suffering, and intransigence can sometimes help avoid it. Neither norm links, necessarily, to "toughness" or "softness": you can be intractable but still soft toward others whose well-being would be shattered by compromising away their interests; and you can be "tough," as with post-9/11 detainees and suspected terrorists, by flexibly equivocating on long-established protections of such people. By the time we find that "we have compromised our basic values," as President Obama stated in late May of 2013, we may have inflicted tough harm on innocents.

Contemporary politics, as well as very long-term history, preoccupy these pages, which state an approach to issues that will delight some on the left as often as it may discourage them. Intransigence is not always, and certainly not solely, a characteristic of conservatives, whom I call here "red-staters." Yet it is often true that "blue-staters" tend to tar highly nuanced positions on the right with the brush of "inflexibility," a label that conveniently forestalls more serious thinking about actual substance.

Whatever their stance on specific issues, the inflexible are much slower than the flexible to deviate from patterns of tradition and experience to which they were already wedded. They have often had to work hard, and this work is described here, to resist the dominant impulse around them to shift rapidly to a new set of judgments. Throughout this book I admire their steadfastness and see advantages in dogmatic positions taken overtly even by those with whom we sharply disagree. Our opponents' willingness to display their passionate beliefs openly permits us to respond better to them than if they masked their dogma behind a rhetoric of compromise. What we then do to oppose them is up to us, but our response should not traduce our own deepest values.

Can a rigorous allegiance to what one already believes sometimes be the wise approach? The book offers a sustained affirmative answer to that question.

Meanwhile the flexible take some pride in their ability to move off fixed positions in the direction of compromise and almost constant change. The fatality of flexibility consists in making flexibility itself a norm of behavior. Ironically, the only faith that cannot be compromised away is the belief in flexibility.

That belief, and the practices it engenders, span two millennia of Western thought, writing, and action. So deeply embedded in so many of us as to preclude self-criticism, the norm of openness to the new, and skepticism about the old, is taught early and effectively. It is part of our formation, both religious and secular, inclining us toward almost limitless change and muting our awareness of flexibility's risks. Those wishing to remain steadfast, through thick and thin, find themselves at the margins. Whatever the merits of their dearly held positions, they are ridiculed or attacked as fanatical, stubborn, intractable, or dogmatic. Some version of these traits, or even all of them together, however, do not always produce extreme or aberrational behavior. Sometimes—indeed often—the limitlessly flexible, and not those intransigent others, provide an extreme reversal of a previously cherished tradition. The European continent, from Berlin to Paris to the British Channel Islands, managed during the Third Reich to compromise its deepest values and to accept—with little effective protest—the new conditions set down by a madman. A precious minority of the steadfast declined, at some risk, to cave. Most people folded their tents and equivocated their way toward active or passive participation in a genocide.

The secular and the religious combine, perhaps only in this way, to promote flexibility and to denigrate its opposite. Malleability and a willingness to compromise even deeply held positions are admired outgrowths of the neo-classical Enlightenment (ch. 3). But there are risks here, even grave risks, and the secular Enlightenment is not their sole source. Flexibility, and an intolerance for fixed positions, began much earlier than several centuries ago, and emerged powerfully from writers at the time of Jesus. The first influence against sticking to belief and tradition is that of the first Christians, including the brilliant Jewish writers St. Paul and St. John. They felt it necessary to commandeer long-standing Jewish traditions and to distort their meanings so that the claims they were making for their new religion could be found in the Jewish sacred texts. For their project to succeed against all the textual odds required not only a maximum of interpretive flexibility but also—tragically—the deliberate denigration of all those who wished to stay true to their laws, their customs, and their way of behaving with others (ch. 3).

This was a terrible mistake. Although individual Christian stalwarts are among the heroes of this book (ch. 4), a certain baleful skepticism about steadfastness emerges from the early Christian writings and remains with us in both religious and secular contexts (ch. 6). This book traces to the very present day the fraught outcome of the confluence of the flexible in our religious and secular heritage. With some attention to the ubiquity of compromise during World War II, which is textually traced in part to the flexible acceptance by the Catholic Church of European anti-semitism, I also focus on contemporary politics. I argue that the equivocation of some of our great constitutional and moral practices derives from 2,000 years of tolerance for a program of quick departures from established meanings and traditions. Flexibility has been a norm in the interpretation of constitutional texts, most recently in the US Supreme Court's approach to the Second Amendment.

Mistakes that can be sourced to 2,000 years ago are still being made as this book is completed, in the crucial development of policies connected to post-9/11 practices such as torture, detention, eavesdropping, and targeted killings, practices that have required extreme flexibility toward long and sound traditions, even as they purport to be pragmatic adjustments to our new century's dominant "emergency."

This book urges its readers to apply any pride of place remaining in their own flexibility to an extended critique of that pride.

Sag Harbor, NY
January 2014

Acknowledgments

The writer is thankful to individuals and institutions whose encouragement and criticism have nurtured this project: the audience at lectures at Yale's Whitney Humanities Center; workshops at Princeton and the University of Illinois, Chicago Circle; the legal theory workshops at Cardozo, Columbia, and Georgetown law schools; the detailed scrutiny of sections of the manuscript by Eric Freedman, Jonathan Weisberg, Sanford Levinson, David Cole, Leon Morris, and Anthony Werner; and the moral support of my late brother, David B. Weisberg, and my wife, Cheryl. To the many students and professional audiences that engaged my Guernsey exercise, described in Chapter 4, notes 16 and 23, goes my gratitude, which extends to my generous institutional home base, the Cardozo Law School of Yeshiva University, and to the Board of Governors of the Law and Humanities Institute. Finally, without the steadfast assistance of Bonnie Farquhar-Charles, Todd Grabarsky, Stephanie Spangler, and Alyssa Grzesh, this book could not have been launched.

IN PRAISE OF
INTRANSIGENCE

1

Thinking About the Way We Think

How Flexibility Can Be Fatal

a. The Micro- and Macro-Level Responses to a Crisis

This book is about the downside of flexibility. That quality, seemingly admirable, has not fared well over the long course of history. Our mainstream traditions, both secular and religious, have given us, each in their separate ways, an almost limitless capacity to see the world elastically; they teach us to fold our tents, through a near endless capacity to compromise even what every fiber of our mature brain matter knows to be correct, especially when a "crisis" calls our values into question. These traditions teach us to yield precisely at times when firmness is required. They teach us harmful lessons about effective and moral action in the world. We begin to misperceive our surroundings and to make terrible mistakes.

The opposite of flexibility is an equal but opposite conditioned reflex, an *advanced intuition* practiced by a small minority of people in our circles of thought these days to avoid such mistakes. These are the "intransigent ones." They can be awfully wrong at times, but then so can the flexible majority. They can be right, too: it is they who stood up to Hitler while most others compromised. They know, through observation, experience, and reflection, that they may have to call on habituated patterns of coolness under fire that context and surroundings will challenge to the fullest. In "emergencies," which have become the norm, their steadfastness deserves admiration, and not only after the fact of the so-called crisis. It has been they, most recently since the tragic events of September 11, 2001, intransigent people on the right as much as on the left, who provide an unwavering allegiance to pre-9/11 traditions that have been negotiated away by flexible politicians and analysts of all persuasions.

To combat the habit of a compromised falling off from long patterns of sound behavior, these people train themselves to think within fearful and contentious situations before they act in the standard way of yielding to the new and often unwise. They stand firm, or in the words of the neuroscientists, they use "metacognition"—they *think about thinking*, digging deep and finding a reserve of calm—an "aequanimitas"[1] where the rest of us have been trained to yield to the exigencies of emotion, conformity, and compromise. They do so not only in their own living rooms, where adherence to principle is less risky and often privately admired, but also in public, the only place that needs intractable talk and sometimes action when sound behavior is otherwise negotiated away.

These people reverse the baseline tendency of the majority, who have been conditioned to give ground. Even when pursuing their steadfast practices in an unassuming manner, as most of them do until directly challenged by events, they may tend to annoy the "pragmatic" and accepting majority who resent not so much their substantive positions as the distractingly living proof they offer of consistency and integrity. Agree or disagree with the actual merits of their views on any given specific issue, we may not like such people, because their firmness alone stupefies us. Only after the fact of their self-assertiveness do they sometimes get the credit they were not even seeking during the crisis itself. What appeared to us in the heat of the emergency as an almost mindless unwillingness to compromise gets trans-valued later, as we look back at those who did not deviate from what we, pre-crisis, always knew was the correct path.

If I use the pronoun "we," it is because this book focuses less on the psychology of any individual actors—call it the "micro"—than on slowly developing patterns of social behavior—call it the "macro."[2] Neither exceptional heroism nor personal fear is at the center of this analysis; we may not all be Chesley Sullenbergers, although people looking carefully at his aircraft-saving "delib-erate calm" conclude that we do in fact possess the organic ca-pacity to draw closer to his example.[3] Practice, it turns out, is key to a calm adherence to the proven good.

Most examples of counter-flow steadfastness in these pages in-volve people who do not think of themselves as particularly "heroic" or in any way extraordinary. To the contrary, they see as "natural" their own sound responses and count on parallel behavior from their friends and colleagues. They call not on idiosyncratic flashes of courage but rather on unfashionable or mislabeled counter-traditions that have been placed unacceptably at risk and need to be redeemed and restored rather than negotiated and compromised.

On the other side of the coin, fear and similarly individual-ized explanations doubtless play some role when so many, so often in history, fail to heed the call of the steadfast. I argue that fear, inspired by a sense of emergency (often exaggerated), de-prives people of the mature judgment that otherwise would guide them wisely through the crisis. However, when we recog-nize how a small minority of ordinary people in every crisis finds a way to act soundly, and when we are learning that we can practice overcoming such fears, the place of long-standing social—rather than individualized—forces emerges more clearly and deserves close examination.

Little in our flexible and pragmatic sense world attracts us to steadfastness, which very often presents to our liberal imaginations as "stubbornness" and an unwillingness to "change." Almost anything that smacks of obstinacy is going to be unpopular, particularly when people think they are in the throes of an emergency, of some defining event or crisis that appears to require quick change from prior baselines. Yet we will find on closer examination that the intransigent few may just be asking for a preservation of what those caught in an anxiety-ridden willingness to compromise also cherish.

Indeed, *restoration of the demonstrably good*, rather than constant, fluid change, is at the heart of this counter-tradition.

Like most of my readers, or so I would imagine them, I was brought up to scorn those who will not compromise what they have concluded to be right. I am a secularist. An entire tradition of enlightened thought, coupled with the comfort most of us feel with permeability and change, positioned me to reject even a whiff of doctrinal or behavioral "rigidity." Some of this aversion is casual and relatively insignificant: on the micro level, no one wants a personality defined by others (especially one's shrink) as "rigid," and we generally do not like dealing with such personalities, either. Yet there are some recent, highly respected thinkers, such as Elaine Scarry, who counsel us to see the value, even of individualized "rigidity" (or Dr. William Osler's "immobility") in some situations of communal need.[4]

Some distaste for the seemingly "rigid" personality is shared more widely. In the media, few appreciate the monomaniacal bloviating of broadcast chatterers, unless, occasionally, their perspective flatters our own. We may, depending on our perspectives, eschew watching the inflexibly right-of-center Fox TV commentators while also telling ourselves that keying in to the uniformly blue-state views of, say, Rachel Maddow, constitutes a form of political activism.

But in these pages, I take the longer view. I evoke those who, through history, have managed to stand fast against foul winds of unwise and overhasty change and consistently to propound beliefs they hold dear, beliefs previously shared by most but then utterly compromised in the name of some needed change occasioned by a perceived or actual crisis. These are not talk show hosts with single constituencies; they are the righteous ones whose audience is their own heart and whose admirers, if usually only in the long run, are all of the rest of us.

Admiration, if it ever reaches the steadfast, comes very slowly, and rarely in their lifetimes. Even the twentieth century's greatest moral crisis, the caving of most of Europe to Hitler's dreadful policies, has left subsequent generations confused about strongly held opinions and beliefs. Within the still-living memory of some of my readers, Hitler's fanatical rhetoric reenforced a sense among many that we simply "never again" wish to hear anything—*anything*—propounded with the fierceness that is associated with those terrible times.

Blunt, unyielding rhetoric is disdained by some otherwise superb thinkers, but this is the wrong lesson to have derived from the Hitler period. The paradox I explore through historical example in these pages is that it was precisely the few *outspoken, clear, and rhetorically strong opponents* of Hitler who might have reversed the course of history if the more moderate among their listeners had heeded their unambiguous and unyielding calls to resist. Straight talk was missing where it was most needed. Instead, the multitudes—the tens of millions of ordinary Europeans who began by detesting Hitler or his surrogates outside of the Reich—displayed the quite common ability to negotiate away their own deepest beliefs and traditions. As we shall see, the best moral influences upon them—say, their own parish priests every Sunday—used at best a "coded" (indirect) language if they said anything at all about the "Jewish question."[5] It is this limitless rhetorical and behavioral *flexibility* (rather than its opposite) that might have been called into question in our postwar responses to Hitler.[6]

Even the dictionary seems to dislike those who publicly buck the trend and decline to conform. The richness of the mother tongue stacks the deck against overly strong contrarian positions openly propounded. The thesaurus links "intransigence" to a whole host of words that codify our distaste for programmatic loyalty to fixed positions: intractable, stubborn, Pharisaic, close-minded, and stiff-necked, to name only a few derogatory synonyms. Such words set up a boundary between the "righteous"—usually perceived as "*self*-righteous"—and us. Usage in speaking about them always inclines us toward such pejoratives as "dogmatic," "hardnosed," "unyielding," "rigid," or "fanatical." I reverse the value, throughout this book, of these negative-seeming traits. I write in praise of intransigence and the many words aligned to it in common parlance.

Very recent experience only exacerbates our distaste for firmness of position. How do we think and feel after the terrible events of 9/11? Moderates otherwise unlikely to throw stones at anyone have made an exception for suspected terrorists, who seem to embody the very illness we detest: fanaticism itself. In the face of such a grave threat, boldly pursued by intractable others, we have resorted to compromising some of our own finer and previously ensconced traditions. This book wonders out loud about the pathways US policy has forged across political divides—pathways that required a good deal of flexible compromise in mapping deviations from sound pre-9/11 mutual understandings of right and wrong. Paradoxically, flexibility leads as often as its opposite to "toughness" against perceived enemies; the question to be asked is whether one or the other tends to lead to sound outcomes consistent with the baseline values that are revived when the crisis has passed.

I started to criticize my own vaunted open-mindedness when I saw the taboo on torture quickly equivocated by some of my closest colleagues. Is there a line between flexible compromise of values and the surrender of what makes those values worth fighting for? I thought a lot about what history teaches, reasonably often, when good people fail to assert their unyielding commitment to long-standing traditions of sound policy. I have become more skeptical of my own flexibility and the effects it has on my actions or nonactions. Some ingrained but unpracticed part of me, something that always realized that constant compromise can be very bad, began to reassert itself. And it reemerged not so much due to very recent compromises on eavesdropping, torture, extreme rendition, unlimited detentions, and targeted killings, but to my growing awareness of millennia-long attitudes that needed examination.

I came to understand that a serious mistake was made 2000 years ago, one that still plagues us today. The error, religious in nature, found a variant in the Enlightenment tradition of such secular thinkers as John Stuart Mill.[7] Both traditions, although otherwise opposed, ask us to understand the world flexibly. Both are joined at the hip precisely in their aversion to strongly held positions that can be characterized as inflexible. The Enlightenment pushes us to test repetitively our own embedded values, even or especially against opposed positions that we think are false; the first Christians showed us how to invade and to distort with infinite flexibility the tenets dearly held by others and then to tar those others with the brush of rigid blindness when they simply held fast to their positions. Eventually, elasticity overwhelmed us, and our own dearest beliefs became slippery and negotiable. We need to understand better how a religious perspective—not *all* religious perspectives, but some that are very familiar to my readers—dovetails with liberal malleability to produce recurring disasters.

b. The Early Jesus Movement's Still-Influential Flexibility

My transformation emerged from a growing understanding that flexibility has a long and identifiable history, one that is hardly edifying. Compromise with accuracy and reason has occurred throughout time, but it was through the putatively Jewish up-starts St. Paul and St. John, that limitless flexibility was formally set down as a good thing and its opposite struck down as bad. These men were trying to form a new faith, one that had much beauty and appeal, yet they felt a need to embed those new faith claims in older Jewish sacred texts whose meanings opposed what they were proclaiming as Gospel. Since all texts, however, are always open to reinterpretation, they at first hoped to find in their fellow Jews a flexible acceptance of more than a few wildly imaginative interpretations of the Jewish Bible. When this largely did not happen—when the claim that Jesus-as-Messiah was prefigured in various passages in the Tanakh, for example, fell largely on indifferent ears—they went a step further, and this is the crucial step for my thesis: they programmatically set down in their own new texts a constant, violent verbal barrage against those who simply declined to see things their way or to compromise the most powerful strains of their own traditions.

The early Jesus movement needed to ensconce a new princi-ple, interpretive malleability, as the very means to create its reli-gion. The entire Hebrew Bible was cannon fodder, and a superb set of texts was distorted to find something in them that literally defied belief! These outrageous interpretations of whole seg-ments of the Jewish Bible required a maximum level of interpre-tive freedom, a program that privileged the very idea of infinite flexibility. History discussed in these pages indicates that such interpretive distortion was written into the very fabric of Catho-lic Church doctrine and directly affected events until the present day. The Catholic Church's own present crisis can be sourced in part to the compromising, rather than the traducing, of some its own dearest values—love for the least powerful, such as children; but those mistaken shifts follow from an even deeper and foundational norm: limitless flexibility in the implementation of its best traditions.

The credo of limitless malleability permitted the compromising of sacred texts 2000 years ago and of sacred principles throughout the ages and into the modern era.

To elevate distortion to the level of a program, powerful writers and their allies in the early Jesus movement employed two tactics that have become all too familiar in contemporary secular contexts. First, they claimed that an "emergency" (the End of Days) mandated a radical undermining of long-established norms. Second—and this was their signally unique contribution to morals—they repetitively attacked the keepers of the older traditions, those who declined their invitation to plunder sacred texts in search of radically new textual meanings, those for whom interpretation could not so grossly exceed certain established and acceptable limits. Jews, or some specifically detested subset, who resisted or ignored the Jesus movement's invasion of their Bible were among the first victims of these flexible name callers. The label "Pharisee," defined empathetically by Harold Bloom as "an ancient Jewish sect that emphasized sanctifying ('strict') interpretation and observance of Mosaic law"[8] was not only laid upon all nonaccepting Jews, sometimes also pilloried as "Judaeans," but also made *morally* bad.

The thing these writers saw as insidious in the old system was not its being unfaithfully followed, but the opposite: these Pharisees (or Judaens, or whichever target subgroup the new texts were using), these resisting ones were *too wedded* to their traditions, their laws, their interpretive constraints. The Jews were not so much accused of *hypocrisy* as *fidelity!* Much more central and narratively enforced time and again, as I shall show, was the equation of "Pharisaism" with a set of morally bankrupt blinders that kept the *old* from seeing and then accepting the *new*. Billions of people around the world to this very day read the astonishing words of these brilliant first Christians. People learn the lessons early, and one that has perhaps not been sufficiently emphasized is that—apart from a central belief based on faith—all traditions and ensconced practices should be negotiable, always. As I shall demonstrate, this became the most salient form of "antisemitism" practiced by Catholic institutions upon Jews during the Holocaust; it was not so much racism for most Europeans, but a by then long ensconced "anti-Talmudism"—a virulent distaste for those who remain loyal to a detailed set of textual traditions that enrich not only their spiritual lives but their everyday dealings with themselves and others.

Paul's self-promulgated "emergency" gave an edge to his claim that the new set of interpretations and the new belief system superseded and rendered morally barren what these resisting Jews insisted on steadfastly retaining:

> Do not be carried away by all kinds of strange teachings; for it is well for the heart to be strengthened by grace, not by regulations about food, which have not benefited those who observe them.... For here we have no lasting city, but we are looking for the city that is to come. (Hebrews, 13: 9–14)[9]

Thus were the intricate and ethically sound laws of *kashruth* disposed of as both unhelpful to anyone and picayune more generally given the imminence of the world's end-time.

The prophesied "emergency," however, never took place—the secular city endured. The world did not end; what endured was these writers' assurance about the elasticity of texts and the moral baseness of sticking to tradition. They had rejected outright, or at a minimum compromised, the value of those practices closest to them, so why would any adherent to any system except their own ever again be honored? Those less flexible were admonished as one variety or another of "Pharisees" (paradoxical, since Jesus was one and Paul was probably trained as one!) and, in more secular times, those who have acted like them in many historical contexts have been similarly tarred.

In this book, I show that a touch of Pharisaic intransigence has characterized most beneficial responses to the incursions of flexible power. I will wonder about the turn to excess manipulation and malleability throughout Western history and contrast it to the rare surviving examples of intractable behavior and ethics. I argue that excess flexibility leads, in times of crisis and often more generally, to disaster.

As this book goes to press, a form of poetic justice seems to be developing. The Catholic Church—the rock of St. Peter—seems to be crumbling. Pope Francis, by all accounts a fine man, faces daunting challenges. Those who pinned the labels "Pharisaic" and "blind" on the steadfast few now face retribution (or at least declining numbers of the faithful) for the very flexibility that led them to see evil in those wishing only to stick to their traditions. The crisis in the church arises not only because of a few unbending, archaic traditions; the church's failure to *adhere* to its finest traditions is bringing it down. As I shall discuss at some length, during World War II, the church stated openly that the compromising by Catholic leaders in Vichy France of its own (anti-racist) doctrine was permissible because of political context and change in Hitler's Europe; so today we are finding that the awful traducing of basic ethical values when children are abused and abusers are protected follows inevitably from within an institution so used to violating its own doctrine that the violations have *become* doctrine. Hypocrisy, again, is not quite the right word; compromise long ago became an ensconced principle to which fealty has been paid all too often.

Flexibility had always been key to Christianity's early and increasingly successful manipulations of Jewish sacred texts; flexibility alone permitted the church in Hitler's Europe specific license to violate its own doctrine by remaining silent, or—as we shall see in Chapter 4—affirmatively condoning in the name of realpolitik a policy of direct racial persecution. Flexibility more recently has allowed the church to sacrifice the welfare of children on the altar of self-protective secrecy.

When brilliant writers set in motion 2,000 years of hatred toward those inclined to stick to fine traditional practices and meanings, they served their own cause well but almost fatally destabilized our cultural traditions. Examples within recent memory are plentiful and disturbing and they are hardly limited to the persecutions throughout history of the "People of the Book."[10] Yet, as to those first community-wide victims of excessive flexibility, I will show how the early Jesus movement continued to affect events directly during World War II. At the onset of the Third Reich, a series of "emergencies," many (like the Reichstag fire) probably scripted by Hitler, frightened all but the most dogmatic into yielding their dearly held positions. Gradually, enlightened people as well as virulent racists came to tolerate genocide. Those who, organically, could not adjust to the grotesque new system became the precious few who resisted it. They were intransigent in their adherence to the best humane values of the great old Continent. Some of them, influenced by their Protestant beliefs, would not compromise those values, and they acted, usually at peril of their lives, careers, and fortunes. Most others caved, not only in Nazi Germany itself but during the four dark years of Vichy France and the five less-well-known years of the British Channel Islands, all of which I shall discuss in these pages. Every trained intuition the French people had proudly displayed regarding equality under law was compromised through a process that once again institutionalized—with the help of Paul and Peter's successors in the church at its highest levels—the flexible betrayal of that fine tradition under law.[11] Just to the west of France, a group of occupied islands in the English Channel such as Guernsey saw British traditions of fairness and due process challenged by racial laws, whose victims counted on steadfast protection but, as we shall see, usually found themselves instead adrift in a sea of malleable compromise.

c. Immediate Advantages of a Move Toward Intransigence

My lifelong habit of easy malleability came not from theology but instead from our liberal, Enlightenment tradition, as refined elegantly by my generation's most influential intellectual movement, usually styled "deconstructionism." I was influenced not only by John Stuart Mill but also by two of my doctoral-level teachers, Paul de Man and Geoffrey Hartman. Each in his *very* different way, these European-born scholars were directly affected by the Holocaust in Europe; they conveyed to their many students a subtle dislike for the "grand narratives" both within cultures and individual lives, for any "pinning down" of meaning, and in some ways even for the quest to articulate reality clearly. These two were among the dominant deconstructionists, and now the succeeding generation to that movement gradually but inevitably is making its way back to St. Paul—deconstructionism, as I argued awhile ago, was new wine in old bottles.[12]

It was soothing to think of myself as endlessly open, quintessentially tolerant, infinitely alive to "new" ideas and skeptical of the *old*. I changed; maybe my acquired trait of flexibility helped me move back to something even deeper in me that needed rediscovery. The key was in overcoming a kind of self-satisfied sense that inflexibility means thoughtlessness. (Both the flexible and the inflexible are capable of great thought as well as thoughtless foolishness. Neither category dictates either outcome.) I now admire those intransigent ones, even where I may disagree with them, who have reflected deeply on the risks of malleability and change for its own sake. Some, like Martin Luther King Jr. (MLK), have spoken publicly about staying true to a set of beliefs and practices needed to avoid what he called the "relativism" of the age. I agree with what MLK stood for and quote him often in this book. I disagree, on the other hand, with Barry Goldwater but will also cite him to the same effect. Indeed, I am not counseling my readers to shift their basic positions on key issues to those intransigently on the right or left; rather I ask you to recognize the validity of a common position they take toward intractability and against infinite elasticity.

Like such people, I began to fathom the awful downside of limitless equivocation and grew weary of flexibility and its frequent ally, compromise. I have caught the contagion of their constant self-discipline. Becoming less inclined to nod agreement at just those times when I most want to shout out "No!" runs the risk of being grouped with religious fanatics, right-wing radio hosts and stringent National Rifle Association opponents of most forms of gun control. Careful, though! Moving toward inflexibility decidedly does *not* entail accepting the positions I hate—quite the contrary; but it has forced me to become more informed about those positions and not simply to reject them because they are propounded dogmatically. It induces me to speak up and act in the direction of my own inner beliefs.

This book aims to convince you that a resistance to limitless compromise might have improved many contemporary and historical events with which you are quite familiar. I urge on you three interrelated benefits of seeing the world less flexibly. In reverse order of importance, intransigence

1. removes the easy out of attacking our *opponents' inflexibility* instead of answering their substantive arguments forcefully with some forceful words and actions of our own;
2. crystallizes our own substantive positions for us and makes us far more effective in battling those whose beliefs or politics or behavior we dislike, since we strive to see their views clearly and insist that they grapple with ours; and
3. forces us, particularly in times of perceived "emergency" or "crisis," to hold fast to our best and deepest values rather than to compromise them flexibly as has happened so often in history.

Point 1 asks you to see that little is gained by rejecting opponents' positions because they seem inflexible. My colleagues, friends, and I rarely need to make judgments about the *substance* of a dogmatic person's point of view: if we can say with some assurance that she maintains her position unyieldingly, we have scored enough points to stop thinking about the issue itself. In religion, fundamentalists of otherwise totally different beliefs are lumped together because they are intractable. Although Orthodox Jews have very little in common with devout Catholics, or Muslim clerics with southern Baptists, they all go into the pot labeled "uncompromising" and the specifics of their belief systems thus more easily are scanted or ignored. But one's own inflexibility actually opens the door to greater understanding of different dogmas because it checks the easy move made just by asserting that another argument has been propounded "uncompromisingly."

In law, "strict construction" of the Constitution seemed the last bastion of a few narrow minds who wished to turn back the clock of progress, until we came to realize that much of what we questioned (*Plessy v. Ferguson* [race]; *Schenck v. US* [free speech]; *Everson v. N.J.* [church/state]; *DC v. Heller* [gun control]) was propounded by judges with an *insufficiently* "strict" sense of constitutional meaning. I will discuss some famous and infamous examples of important cases that went terribly wrong because courts flexibly distorted constitutional meanings and then had to be corrected by the hard work of smart people who intransigently demanded a restoration of the text's proper meaning. Some succeeded in doing so; others may still be struggling for what they view as sound.

In politics, debates are stunted on issues ranging from abortion to the teaching of evolution to global warming to universal health care, as progressives lecture opponents not so much on the wrongness of their arguments as on their *rigidity* in propounding them. The Republicans are less flexible than the Democrats, so the latter make that trait a talking point instead of more single-mindedly espousing the substance of their own liberal beliefs. There is something soothing about labeling positions opposed to our own as "uncompromising." While the inflexible often tend more to fight their religious or political battles on the issues, the first and sometimes final claim of flexible folk is that such people "just will not see any other point of view."

The second benefit opens the screen to welcoming, rather than scorning, the intractability of our opponents. It is only when silly or abhorrent positions are placed clearly on the table by inflexible adversaries that we rise up either to insist on change or to rally for the preservation of excellent traditions that they are now undermining. But to do this, we must welcome their passion and not denigrate it. Progressive change usually occurs after those who would block it become completely open—unabashedly uncompromising—about their beliefs. The civil rights movement gained momentum after Americans saw with their own eyes Bull Connors's dogs fleshing out the segregationist position on the bodies of civil rights activists; then—and not with the Supreme Court decision years earlier in *Brown v. Board*—did we work zealously to bring about progress.

By contrast, we sometimes fail to resist bad changes when those bringing them about cleverly conceal their aims and seem to be conciliatory. They hide their illiberality from us, and we are distracted by their temporary masks of even-handedness and compromise. How many Germans were deceived, during the transition to Hitler in 1932–33 by the Nazi party's seeming (but short-lived!) adoption of parliamentary democracy. In the post-9/11 world, it has been the secret memos, not the overt articulation of policy, that have brought about targeted killings, torture, wiretapping, and other "flexible" incursions upon some of our deepest constitutional traditions. So we begin to welcome the overt indication of views we oppose, rather than to seek solace in what are often deceptive signs of compromise on the other side.

It is much better to have an openly inflexible opponent, but only if we simultaneously jettison this aversion to hard-nosed positions of our own. Violence from fanatical others is, of course, a risk at the extremes of human intransigence. But this book everywhere will indicate that untold violence to innocent others arises from compromise and flexibility at least as much as from intractability. Facing threats forthrightly and diligently, an inflexible individual or movement can forestall the violence that an adversary's overt show of unacceptable behavior helps us to discern.

My third and most significant point indicates that a willingness to embrace inflexibility releases us from a consistently elastic discourse—"well, sure, you make a good point there, too!"—to one that recognizes we have beliefs *worthy of uncompromising articulation*. This approach sharpens our finest intuitions and translates them into the domain of words and occasionally actions that bring about change when it is needed but can also preserve excellent traditions that have been placed at risk. My examples range historically across the 2000-year battle between steadfastness and flexibility, culminating in descriptions of the former through rare examples of resistance to Hitler and of the latter through recent contortions of law in White House memoranda justifying torture, drone killings, and other departures from long-held and excellent traditions.

We now know that the subtle and not so subtle post-9/11 changes in American tradition crossed party lines and revealed something deeper than mere "red-state" *versus* "blue-state" differences. I noticed my like-minded liberal law school colleagues equivocating on 9/12 about torture, limitless detention, and the elimination of judicial oversight. I reminded them, in conversations and on the written page, that on 9/10 such practices were anathema to them. "Emergency"—the factor that most brings out our own fears and phobias—pushes us further into pliability and compromise. We are moved, until we think harder about it, to give up our soundest beliefs because—or so most people seem to say when caught up in an "emergency"—in a supposedly ever-changing world, adherence to principle makes no sense.

When we shift from a norm of negotiability and constant change to one of greater confidence in what we believe, we do run the risk of feeling that we are joining forces with hardnosed groups and people whose intransigence we are trained to dislike. Maybe we will end up not only by being like them in this one way, but also by adopting their actual views. There lies the fallacy that keeps so many right-minded folks from returning to what they hold dear. They must first shake off the *Zeitgeist* of relativism that has only rarely been challenged by those we tend to admire.

One of these uncompromising ones was Martin Luther King Jr. He counseled reflection, retention, and restoration. The change he looked for was back in the direction of the finest beliefs we had always held but had somehow lost. His speeches strove to preserve what had been fine but then degraded; he urged us to stick to the program, against the constant winds of change and uncertainty that distracted us.

Obviously, his was a kind of biblical appeal, yet it resonated with people of many faiths and political perspectives.

Guided by the programmatic steadfastness of Martin Luther King Jr., audiences saw that the good usually reemerges clearly from the fog of the new and untested. In a speech to the Lansing (Michigan) National Association for the Advancement of Colored People (NAACP) delivered in a Detroit church in 1954, King codified a form of righteous intransigence into his title, "Rediscovering Lost Values." With a characteristic nod to the Jewish prophetic tradition, he moved from the felt assumption that "there is something wrong with our world" to the surprising conclusion that to change things we need not move to the new and popular but rather *back* to the tried and true:

> My friends, all I'm trying to say is that if we are to go forward today, we've got to go back and rediscover some mighty precious values that we've left behind....I'm not so sure if we know that there are moral laws just as abiding as the physical law. [W]e have adopted in the modern world a sort of relativistic ethic....Most people can't stand up for their convictions, because the majority of people might not be doing it. And, since everybody else is doing it, it must be right.[13]

King often cited the Jewish biblical texts in his speeches, and the yearning for justice that uniquely pervades those stories fit well with his nonviolent but still somehow martial rhetoric. In the Detroit speech, however, a lovely story of loss and return from the *New* Testament fulfilled his theme. He describes Jesus, Mary, and Joseph traveling together to Jerusalem for Passover; when the parents then head back to Nazareth, they discover they have left Jesus behind—"they had lost a mighty precious value. They had sense enough to know that before they could go forward to Nazareth, they had to go backwards to Jerusalem to rediscover this value." True to the text as he was to his movement, King builds on a story and remains faithful to it, affirming his dominant theme.

In using stories from both the Christian and Jewish Bibles, MLK awoke audiences in the 1950s and 1960s who were otherwise skeptical of religious discourse in the public arena. His rhetoric was uncompromising, but the religious component inspired rather than threatened. This, too, constituted a "return," a move back to a tradition of soundness in grasping textual meanings from both Judaism and Christianity and in asking his listeners to translate the ancient stories into current moral and political improvement. MLK partook more of the Jewish prophetic tradition, at least in this sense, and his speeches went "backwards" to practices many others in the Christian world had lost to flexibility over the millennia.

To find the counter-flow minority position against compromise, we must be willing to buck many trends, some as new as the latest source of chatter and others, which I will show, as old as the Jesus stories MLK retold so compellingly to his Michigan audience in 1954. We should "move back" to some older stories, but these may need to be recast creatively. So, I introduce early in these pages a new word—"flexiphobia"—and a new name for the less compromising among us: "flexiphobes." They practice an aversion to compromise the way others practice weightlifting. Without frequent thinking and reinforcement, too much in the air around would move them to quick abandonment of sound positions.

Not surprisingly, a secular literary tradition of great force and merit supports this preservation of sound instincts in the face of circumstances that lead flexible folks astray. Often, we see our great fiction writers reminding us through narrative or essay of what I am calling the need for flexiphobic assertions of what we think to be right; a very recent example is Salman Rushdie:

We find it easier, in these confused times, to admire physical bravery than courage—the courage of the life of the mind, or of public figures. A man in a cowboy hat vaults a fence to help Boston bomb victims, while others flee the scene....Perhaps we have seen too much, grown too cynical about the inevitable compromises of power. There are no Gandhis, no Lincolns anymore.[14]

Shakespeare, in *Hamlet*, offers us the dilemma of flexible analysis tragically substituted for organically justified action by a Prince who, as discussed later in these pages, is less a procrastinator than a compromiser. Closer to home, the twentieth-century American storytellers, Susan Glaspell and William Faulkner challenge readers to see the virtue of what Faulkner's narrative repetitively and positively calls "intractability" in the face of misused power.[15]

Somewhat like the first responders recently described by Elaine Scarry, and also like others who train themselves to think under the stress of the seemingly "new" and exigent,[16] flexiphobes "work out," not physically but intellectually and spiritually, so that when others begin to yield to "changes" they stand up and remind people of what is categorically right and wrong; they administer "CPR" to the failing heart of those easily affected by real or perceived emergencies. They are continuously habituated by their study of history, of stories, and of current events, to stand apart from the intellectual tradition of limitless flexibility, programmatic compromise, and easy distortion of positions once held dear. My book asks you to revalue words like "intractable" and "intransigent" and to make space for this one beleaguered group—perhaps even to join with them.

I begin with a survey of three fascinating recent studies of compromise itself and distance myself in varying degrees from their endorsement of it. As I will try to show, a baseline willingness to compromise follows from the trait of flexibility and carries with it similar risks.

Notes

1. There is an interesting literature across the disciplines regarding the possibility of training ourselves to reach a kind of "equanimity" that helps us to retain what our mature judgment and practice know to be sound, even and especially when emergencies threaten us. William Osler, a renowned turn-of-the-century doctor and humane thinker, "defined 'imperturbability' as 'coolness and presence of mind under all circumstances, calmness amid storm, clearness of judgment in moments of great peril, immobility and impassiveness'" (A. E. Rodin and J. D. Key, "William Osler and Aequanimitas," *Journal of the Royal Society of Medicine* 87 [December, 1994]: 758. See also Donald Kahneman's *Thinking Fast and Slow* [New York: Farrar, Straus and Giroux, 2011], which treats the psychology of "cognitive biases" that adversely affect choices in economics and the world of finance).

My analysis recognizes in various places the empirical work of Elaine Scarry in *Thinking in an Emergency* (Cambridge, MA: Harvard University Press, 2011), a small masterpiece that tracks, empirically, the training for emergencies of communal lifesavers such as first responders.

2. My approach throughout is on the level of the "macro" influences across many centuries, what is generally known as Geistesgeschichte or "longue duree" analysis; see, e.g., Gavin Langmuir, *History, Religion, and Antisemitism* (Berkeley: University of California Press, 1990). I am interested in the cultural forces in the West that have promoted "flexibility" and "compromise" as opposed to steadfastness when people make decisions, particularly in fraught periods they perceive as "emergencies."

3. On Chesley "Sully" Sullenberger, see, e.g., W. Timothy Gallwey, Edd Hanzelik, and John Horton, *The Inner Game of Stress* (New York: Random House, 2009): "What's interesting in the context of stress is that Sully was able to make a complex decision in the face of danger and fear. Pilots call this skill 'deliberate calm.' Because accessing this skill requires conscious effort and regular practice, it is rehearsed over and over again.... What does conscious effort require? [Sully balanced] his automatic emotions with a more rational and deliberate thought process, which is centered in the prefrontal cortex of the brain," pp. 45–46. See also Dr. Neil Singh, who reports that other professionals, such as surgeons, have learned calm and deliberative practices from Sully and

other pilots, "On a Wing and Prayer: Surgeons Learning from the Aviation Industry," *Journal of the Royal Society of Medicine* 102 (September 1, 2009): 360–64. On "deliberate calm" and the frontal cortex, there is a rich scientific literature; on a lay level, see Jonah Lerner, "Capt. Sully and Deliberate Calm," *Los Angeles Times*, January 17, 2009, op. ed.

My own empirical work has tracked the decision making of lawyers in times of crisis. I have concluded that they are not using all available parts of their very fine brains when asked to role-play as wartime lawyers deciding the fate of an allegedly Jewish innkeeper in the occupied British Channel Islands. See Weisberg, "In Defense of 'Flexiphobia': How Training in Intractability Can Help Lawyers in Moments of Perceived Emergency," *Cardozo Law Review* 33 (2012). See also the discussion in Chapter 4, notes 16, 20.

4. Again, Osler, n. 1, and Scarry, *Thinking in an Emergency*:

The procedures for CPR confirm a feature of habit that is often cited in critiques of habit, its

> rigidity, while at the same time vividly illustrating a mistake those critiques make when they attribute to rigidity a robotic (or automaton-like) lack of thought.... The procedures are so well internalized that mental space is left over for addressing additional complicating patterns. (note 1, p. 20)

5. For a detailed study of France's Catholic prelates and parishes during World War II, see Vesna Drapac, *War and Religion: Catholics in the Churches of Occupied Paris* (Washington, DC: Catholic University of America Press, 1998); see further discussion here in Chapter 4 at note 5.

6. See discussion, this volume, Chapter 2 text at note 8.

7. *On Liberty* (1859), especially ch. 2, "Of the Liberty of Thought and Expression": "If all mankind minus one were of one opinion, and only one person were of the contrary opinion, mankind would be no more justified in silencing that one person, than he, if he had the power, would be in silencing mankind.... We can never be sure that the opinion we are endeavoring to stifle is a false opinion: and if we were sure, stifling it would be an evil still." I admire Mill's essay more than do some of its sharper recent critics (see, e.g., Frederick Schauer, *Free Speech: A Philosophical Enquiry* [Cambridge: Cambridge University Press, 1982], ch. 2), but at a minimum its liberal permeability needs to be challenged. First of all, there is the evidence of all of recorded history that truth may never catch up to falsehood or not until it is much

too late; and then there is the contrary philosophical tradition, epito-
mized perhaps by Edmund Burke, who counseled his eighteenth-
century British contemporaries to "revert to your old principles" and
to oppose, for example, taxing the American colonists. Sometimes
what is required to be right is not flexible adaptation of the new but
change in the direction of one's prior sound beliefs. . . . See *The Works and
Correspondence of the Right Honorable Edmund Burke* (III, 1853), pp.
219–20. Martin Luther King agreed in this sense anyway with Burke;
see this chapter, text at n. 13.

8. Harold Bloom, *Jesus and Yahweh* (New York: Penguin Group, 2005).
The Pharisees were one of many Jewish sects at the time of Jesus, and
probably the least likely to oppose new messianic claims such as those
made by Jesus's followers. But the label, thanks to the New Testament,
came to embody everything that was morally wrong with Jewish faith
and law traditions. See, e.g., A. N. Wilson, *Paul: The Mind of the Apostle*
(New York: Random House, 1997), pp. 32–55; James Carroll, *Constantine's Sword* (Boston: Houghton Mifflin, 2001), p. 111.

9. My source for all New Testament citations in this book is Amy-Jill
Levine and Marc Zvi Brettler, *The Jewish Annotated New Testament*
(New York: Oxford University Press, 2011; hereinafter Levine and
Brettler); here p. 425.

10. See Chapter 6 for a discussion of the destabilization of secular law
and its effect on various powerless minorities.

11. Weisberg, *Vichy Law and the Holocaust in France* (New York: New York
University Press, 1996). For other sources, see this book, chapter 4.

12. Weisberg, "Paul, Pomo, and the Legitimacy of Choice Post 9/11,"
Cardozo Law Review 24 (2003): 1615. Postmodernism, for me anyway,
can produce great elegance and complexity but always in the direction
of Pauline flexibility. Among recent thinkers who are identified broadly
with that approach, I would cite here Alain Badiou, a Marxist who
adores St. Paul, to the denigration of other religions including the one
targeted in some of Paul's worst polemics; see, e.g., *Saint Paul: La Fonda-
tion de L'universalisme* (Paris: PUF, 1997).

13. Martin Luther King Jr., "Rediscovering Lost Values," speech to the
Lansing (MI) NAACP, February 28, 1954, delivered at Detroit's Second
Baptist Church.

14. Rushdie, Sunday *New York Times*, April 27, 2013, op. ed., p. 6. Rushdie's
eloquent passage makes me yearn for a 21st-century Israeli Rabin.

15. In Faulkner's *Intruder in the Dust* (New York: Vintage, 1996; first published 1948), the word "intractable" is used seven times, and "inflexible" three more, to describe a black man, unjustly accused of murder, caught in a moment of southern white turmoil and reactive violence. His firmness combines with the uncompromising sense of fairness of three other characters to help prevent his lynching.

16. See sources at notes 1, 3, and 4 this chapter.

2

The Politics of Compromise

"Red-Baiting" Takes a New Form

a. The Easy Out of Labeling Others "Uncompromising"

For a small cadre of people in each generation, a trained organic resistance to compromise sustains their deeply held positions against the majority's willingness to yield when events (as they always do) create new conditions. Although, in the judgment of history, such folks are often redeemed and even revered (dissenters to Hitler's policies; to the incarceration of Japanese-Americans during World War II; to the McCarthy "red scare"), such people are disliked at the time, often for the wrong reason. Of course, sometimes we take umbrage at the *substance* of their positions. For example, post-9/11, Americans do not like Middle Eastern fundamentalists, and the feeling is mutual. Each sees the other as locked into positions that defy political and moral soundness, positions that can only be maintained by a madman.

But it could also be that a predilection to compromise impels the majority to dislike strongly held positions just *because* they are inflexibly maintained. People in certain traditions, including those of mainstream Western thought (religious and secular), reject all rigidly sustained positions, crazy or not-so-crazy. People who remain firm, even if our own better angels think they are probably right, are annoying: like Molière's title character in *Le Misanthrope*, they spread the gloom of reminding us of what we know deep down we should be doing.

In domestic politics, the margin on the actual issues may be far narrower between us and fellow citizens than between us and the Ayatollahs, the North Koreans, or those propounding terror throughout the world. Yet the main problem with our domestic adversaries may remain the same: we don't like noncompromisers. We prefer those who "accommodate" the perspectives of others. And this is because we wish to sustain our habits of thought, which compel us to yield at least some of what we have begun with in order to get some of what we want and at the same time prove our open-mindedness. We call the latter tendency "a willingness to compromise." It is an excellent thing until it becomes its own "fundamentalism," until, that is, it replaces thoughtfulness about issues with a smug sense that all noncompromisers are by definition wrong and that we fulfill our responsibilities just by showing flexibility.

I call our home-grown, fully domestic distaste for noncompromisers "red- baiting." It is an only slightly more flattering mirror image of the old McCarthy era name-calling, but this time the label is affixed by liberals to conservatives. The latter, called "red-staters," find themselves lectured to—for example, during President Obama's first term in office—for being "uncompromising." A few examples come to mind where "blue-staters" such as myself and my friends hectored conservatives not on their actual positions but instead on their fierce unwillingness to negotiate those views. Why won't they come to the table? The question often replaced "What is it about the substance of their positions that I need to think about and respond to?" or even "What more do I need to do to *win* on this issue?"

Meanwhile, on George W. Bush's watch, it was a few conservatives in the Senate and the Army who took the lead in remaining loyal both to our anti-torture taboo and to the already existing Military Code of Justice's constraint on interrogation techniques and limitless detention.[1] More recently, under President Obama, it was it up to Senator Rand Paul to filibuster against CIA director John Brennan's nomination, seeking information about the use of drones.

"Democrats silent" on the issue, said headlines in early March 2013.[2] After all, if any recent set of policies seemed to require "flexible change," post 9/11 anti-terrorist practices filled the bill; and here were these sticks-in-the-mud—these *filibusterers!* (read: red-staters permitted year-after-year by overly flexible Democrats to retain a veto by mustering forty votes)[3] reminding us that some good traditions should not be compromised. They reminded us of existing courts with judicial independence, of laws that limited detention within prescribed periods, of constraints on the executive branch's desire to be judge, jury and executioner in the name of an emergency. Their inclination to stand firmly behind these fine traditions may not always have lasted much longer than ours, and it seems to have motivated Democrats into tradition-restoring action, but it was noteworthy that the provenance of steadfast resistance generally came from "the right."

The torture issue has its variations in the current (liberal) administration. I will discuss the troubling continuation of some policies, including non-transparency, in a later section. For now, though, consider some other arenas in which blue-staters show impatience with rigidly held red-state perspectives. Suppose, for starters, that we have been asked to reckon with the desires of parents in some southern school districts to teach "creationism" along with evolution in public school science classes. One way we can avoid real reflection on the issue would be to tar the southern adherents with the brush of "rigidity," "intransigence," "fundamentalism," and other labels. In fact, as a teacher of the First Amendment, I have been forced to grapple with their position and have learned that—although I still strongly disagree with it—there is much to be said in favor of some red-state parents' arguments on this issue.[4]

Those very parents, and folks with analogous views in other political arenas, generally do not fall back on tarring their opponents as "uncompromising." Second amendment absolutists—with the recent help of the Supreme Court[5] and a typically inactive Senate on both sides of the aisle[6]—propound with annoying obstinacy their substantive sense that the Constitution gives them an individual right to own and use guns for self-defense, just as pro-life people fall back on religious or other baselines, and those who insist on teaching creationism in public schools speak of academic freedom to let students hear "both sides" of the story of how we came to be on earth. They insist on stating, intransigently, their own positions. They rely less on calling their opponents inflexible, as though that were the knockout argument.

Blue-staters tend to ascribe the inability to get things done to their adversaries' failure to compromise, while red-staters generally care more about the substance of the issues and do not mind either side's display of "extreme" support for what they believe. So there is this major difference in the way blue-staters and red-staters contribute to gridlock: to the compromising mind, the red staters are wrong simply because they "refuse to negotiate"; for the intractable ones, the issues need to be volubly and passionately expressed by both sides until one or the other prevails. No wonder most of us prefer compromisers! No wonder the others are cast in somber tones that are, ironically perhaps, biblical in their pejorative force! They are stiff-necked, pharisaic, blind, and impenetrable!

Everything depends, for the minority who tend to hold fast, on the substance of their beliefs. Agree or disagree, they have the integrity of their perspectives in mind. Once I slough off the "red herring" of their failure to compromise, I get to the beef I have with them, and it is refreshing and useful to get to the heart of disagreements and fight hard for the positions I (or you, or most blue-staters) maintain.

Throughout history, it is usually the noncompromisers who stand firm against what everyone afterward knows have been hideous alterations in the basic values of one society or another. The stakes are rarely as high when it comes to political disputes these days; but cosmic or not in its implications, a noncompromising insistence on overt displays of substantive positions, as opposed to procedural deflections into the question of who will compromise first, alerts both sides to what is really going on in their opponents' minds. This is helpful. History demonstrates that as differences approach crisis levels involving issues of great moral, religious, and political consequence, compromisers have not done well. Those situations, which I describe in some detail later, entail the victory of others who single-mindedly further programs we detest while we patiently await some compromise or angrily insist on it. Finally, we propound our own deepest values and begin to fight. By then it is often too late. The willingness—indeed the eagerness—to compromise has long since taken its horrible toll.

b. Three Recent Approaches to Compromise

1. Gutmann and Thompson: Change at all Costs

In a range of assessments of the question of compromise, three recent books cover ground from the ephemeral to the historically significant and ask how a disposition to compromise affects the choices we make.

At a flexible extreme, Amy Gutmann and Dennis Thompson (*The Spirit of Compromise*) try to poke holes in what they call the "uncompromising mindset" (pp. 64–66). Although they attempt to make a distinction between "principles" (which should not be too easily compromised) and "interests" (which should), the attempt is half-hearted and the distinction less well drawn than the analogous "rules-principles" dichotomy I mention regarding the US Constitution in Chapter 6. In fact, they want to chip away even at our most dearly held positions, which they deride under the label "principled tenacity." Their book focuses on contemporary American politics, so it is not surprising that they accuse today's politicians of willfully pushing all interests into the domain of "principle," hence both declining to compromise and sounding virtuous at the same time.

> "I will never compromise my principles." So says nearly every politician running for office or trying to stay in office. (If you doubt the ubiquity of this declaration, just try an Internet search with this phrase and its equivalents.) This declaration displays the first characteristic of the uncompromising mindset—principled tenacity. (p. 69)

Their book everywhere establishes compromise as *its* "principle," and the relatively easy target of American political rhetoric makes that stance topical but perhaps more than a bit ironic. Under these authors' scrutiny, tenacity, except as to a constant willingness to compromise, fares poorly. Yet the authors are uncompromising in their admiration of—and call to—compromise. So their own skepticism about principle leads them to extreme misrepresentations of tenacity, or what I have been calling *intransigence*:

> If all politicians rejected all compromises that violate any of their principles, even when making improvements on the

> status quo required compromise, then no particular compro-
> mise would ever be acceptable. (p. 72)

Unassailable, the statement is also uninteresting, because words
like "all," "any," and "ever" deliberately rob tenacity of its real-
world grit and hence of its potential praiseworthiness. No one
insists on fighting *all* the time, for *any* cause, against *anything*
short of complete victory. On the contrary, the inflexible ones
choose their battles *selectively*, only when they sense that Gutmann and Thompson's "status quo" must be preserved against
what they believe are *unacceptable* calls for change or when they
insist on restoring through political change what they believe
has been *unacceptably* altered, a struggle I soon describe on the
level of Constitutional Law.

In the face of seemingly unyielding opposition that appears
to have some merit, there are few politicians, even among the
tea-party or extreme red-state representatives Gutmann and
Thompson are largely targeting, who will *never* yield some or
even most of their own tenacity. However, this will not take place
when—as in Obama's first term—their opponents lecture them
for being "uncompromising" rather than on the substance of the
policies that divide them. Compromise on difficult issues occurs
*after the articulation of both sides' seemingly intractable perspectives
on the merits*; if one side (as most of history shows) fails to take
strong and even unyielding positions and instead grumbles
that the other side "simply will not compromise" on theirs, the
root issues that divide them, although close to the surface, are
fruitlessly concealed by a discourse of compromise versus non-
compromise. The tenacious holders of views we do not like will
prevail while we weakly decline to pronounce our own opposing
views and instead moan about their lack of flexibility.

The acceptance of compromise as a baseline robs the other
side ("our" side) of the proclivity to plead and prove our own case

as forcefully as we can. I may not like red-state intransigence on climate change, so what do I do about it? Am I to "avoid the uncompromising mindset" and focus either on what I might be able to accept in my opponents' arguments or, since there is nothing there for me to work with, emphasize the intransigent nature of their arguments? Or should I not make the strongest arguments I can, in whatever arenas may help me, to prove that environmental change can and must result from alterations in human behavior?

So Gutmann and Thompson badly misdirect their additional criticism of those whose "mindset" they attack:

> The second characteristic of the uncompromising mindset—mutual mistrust—focuses on the attitude of the agents. Politicians with this mindset speak and act on the assumption that their opponents are motivated mainly by a desire to defeat them and the principles for which they stand. (p. 65)

These words much better describe most "liberals" (including the president during his first term) than the red-staters the authors apparently wish to criticize. Too frequently avoiding the merits of the issues on the table, it was the "compromisers" who always assumed that the motives of their adversaries were by definition suspect: their intractable positions were seen to be exclusively in the service of defeating Obama in the 2012 presidential campaign. No credence was given to the possibility that these uncompromising foes really wanted what they were arguing for (or against), only that their sole motivations were "political."

Seen in the light of the 2012 elections, decided some months before this chapter was written, the weakness of Gutmann and Thompson's attack on principled tenacity in politics becomes clearer. The debate has shifted, most obviously right now to the issues of gun control, immigration, Edward Snowden, and eaves-dropping. Folks are starting to move away from some baseline "compromise" position to the *substance* of the divisive issues. The president on his Health Care program, with some inevitable roll-out slippage, has become the resolute leader I and others admire greatly and has shed some of the professorial inclina-tion to lecture his political foes. If this continues, it will be all to the good for our public deliberations, but the performance de-pends on the president's baseline predilection: flexibility versus leadership.

The key to the perspective of these two authors—as I read them—is a strong normative preference for *changes* in the status quo. I think their readers will be inclined—but only at first—to support such manifestos for change as the following passage:

> The imperative to act and therefore to compromise is not ex-clusively liberal or conservative. Almost no one is satisfied with the way things are. The only reason to privilege the status quo as a general rule is the fatalistic belief that any change is bound to make things worse. In politics, this is not a sustainable position. Even if the laws were to remain the same, the world would change. (p. 211)

I agree with nothing in this passage. Undergirding it are two assumptions: first, Americans favor "change" for its own sake. Very few people, Gutmann and Thompson tell us, are satisfied with the way things *are*. On this account, we unthinkably desire change *all the time*. Like flicking the zapper on our cable televisions, we flit around from where we are to anywhere else—*anywhere* else!

Those who don't want change have an almost irrational faith in the status quo for its own sake, or so Gutmann and Thompson allege. Since change is what we allegedly desire at all times, then there is almost at every moment an "imperative to act," and action requires, or so says the previous passage, compromise. And inaction, they wrongly conclude, follows from faith in the status quo.

By way of answer, the status quo may contain elements that should be relatively impermeable to "change" for its own sake. I've mentioned the pre-9/11 taboo against torture, or pre-World War II Europe's investment in republican democracy and a notion of equality under law, or pre-Christian era readings of the Jewish sacred texts. Should supporters of those traditions automatically open themselves to Gutmann and Thompson's version of status quo skepticism? Should they have "zapped" those values and moved on to others (targeted killings; Hitler's Europe; New Testament commandeering of the older texts) just in the name of change? Though we know this only retrospectively, the answer is "no!" So Gutmann and Thompson are wrong to endorse universal change as a norm of conduct.

Then, too, a refusal to compromise is itself a form of action: it satisfies Gutmann and Thompson's "imperative to act" but it does not do so by zapping to some new status quo. Sometimes the action that is required is *uncompromising* by nature. Think of resistance fighters in World War II Europe, counter-flow thinkers regarding the means we use to conduct the war on terrorism, scholars insisting on the dignity of meanings within their own textual traditions, passive resistance when governments alter traditional understandings of the good.

It is never enough to feel pride in our own willingness to compromise, or at least it is not enough to do this when key matters of morality, religion, and politics are at stake. Gutmann and Thompson endorse compromise for its own sake, so that what we want to accomplish within a given situation takes second place to our desire to show our open-mindedness. When push comes to shove, less permeable people with programs different from our own gain an advantage, History proves that, for better or worse, the key battles are fought and won by the uncompromising. In the long run, sometimes the very long run, the good may overwhelm the bad. It just takes a lot longer for the right position to prevail, because too often those who deserve to prevail lose time proving how flexible they are.

How effective we are likely to be against inflexible others depends in part on a thoughtful redirection of our habits of mind. Permit me an example that illustrates such a redirection. I have conjured earlier in this text the words of Martin Luther King Jr. counseling us to "go back" to what we know is right; now I will cite someone unlikely to be named in the same breath with MLK, Barry Goldwater. In his acceptance speech to the 1964 Republican convention, Goldwater stated "that extremism in the defense of liberty is no vice... [and] that moderation in the pursuit of justice is no virtue."[7] Everybody knew that the Democrats gained victory as soon as this sentence was uttered. The sentiment sounded so bizarre, so off center.

Goldwater lost the rhetorical war and the 1964 election, but he was saying something worth thinking about. In the mouth of an MLK, as we have seen, the same basic idea in his Michigan speech gained prevalence as the tumultuous decade proceeded. Some recourse to fundamentals, they both agreed in sharply different ways, does us good. So what would have been the Vietnam-era policy of a man less given to compromise than LBJ? Would there have been a Gulf of Tonkin incident, which led us into a "wider war"? Would there have been the same looseness of understanding regarding the president's war powers in the first place? Goldwater asserted in another part of the speech, which no one remembers except for its infamous dictum on extremism, that it "has been during Democratic years that we have weakly stumbled into conflict, timidly refusing to draw our own lines against aggression, deceitfully refusing to tell even our people of our full participation, and tragically, letting our finest men die on battlefields, unmarked by purpose, unmarked by pride or the prospect of victory." Maybe he would have insisted on transparency of information and declined to send in more troops (as LBJ did from mid-1965 on) until US goals and capacities were fully vented. But LBJ's campaign handlers painted Goldwater into a radical corner, and their ads depicted him with nuclear explosions in the background. A man of considerable conviction, he may never have taken us into the quagmire, as LBJ eventually did.

I voted for LBJ but then four years later rejoiced when he stepped down after the insurgent I was working for in 1968, Eugene McCarthy, showed remarkable strength in some of the primaries. In 1964, I joined others against Goldwater not only on policy grounds but also because he was seen as a rigid man who would not compromise. And that was the fallacy in my thinking if not in my ultimate vote.

Perhaps we should have engaged Barry Goldwater and others like him on the issues. Extreme disagreement, a product of the uncompromising "mindset" (as Gutmann and Thompson like to call it), is a beneficial outgrowth of a hardening of our substantive positions in the face of equally hard-nosed opponents. Uncompromising opponents rarely remain so if those who feel differently enough about actual issues display the tenacity their beliefs deserve. We should welcome our foes' "principled tenacity," their unyieldingness, for at least two reasons: it gives us an opportunity, on the issues we care most about, to make uncompromising arguments of our own. The battle will be joined on the substance of our difference and not on the sideshow of who is being more flexible. Principled tenacity on both sides, as I have argued, serves further to bring our opponents' positions more clearly to the surface. History shows that opponents who ultimately will fight to the death for views we abhor too often lure us in by the mask of flexibility they put on to reassure us. Hitler had already published *Mein Kampf* with all its unconcealed ranting; but mainstream Germans lost their clear-eyed vision when he put on the compromising disguises of parliamentarian and statesman! Once in power—elected at that!—he reverted to his true nature. And it was too late.

We need to reverse our sometimes smug invocation of flexibility at all costs. Gutmann and Thompson largely flatter that inclination by emphasizing that

> Compromises [even] of principle do not require all or nothing decisions any more than do compromises of interest. Principles can be—and most often are—realized only partially—more or less, not all or nothing. (p. 77)

The problem with this formulation, which may be true as an empirical matter, is that the reader already convinced by it may now elevate it to what its authors otherwise would deride as a "principle," one that differs from all the others because they have told us that it—a willingness to compromise—should *never* be compromised. And that is a bad mistake.

2. Avishai Margalit: Rotten Compromises

More nuanced and interesting, for my purposes at least, is Avishai Margalit's *On Compromise and Rotten Compromise*. Margalit's book starts from a baseline close to mine. Unlike the other books I am discussing, his begins with real skepticism about the urge to compromise. Margalit's examples come not only from recent politics (although he alludes throughout to the Israeli-Palestinian conflict) but also from history. In discussing Winston Churchill, a man rightly renowned for his unwillingness to compromise, Margalit looks back at the 1938 Munich Agreement that in effect gave Czechoslovakia to Hitler in exchange for a promise of peace and the end of all further Nazi territorial demands. His account is typically careful, and first asks whether this agreement constituted "coercion" rather than "compromise." A coerced agreement, in Margalit's always scrupulous analysis, cannot be called a compromise, despite an appearance of give-and-take between the parties to it. Deciding that Munich was in fact a compromise, because the Western leaders such as Neville Chamberlain who negotiated it never felt they were incapable of freely bargaining with Hitler, Margalit clears further ground by confirming the good motives of Chamberlain, whom Churchill himself called an "uncompromising struggler for peace."

> So what is rotten in the Munich pact? My answer is that the one with whom it was signed, and not what was signed, makes it rotten. A pact with Hitler was a pact with radical evil, evil as an assault on morality itself....[W]hat Nazism stood for should have been clear in the thirties: it stood for radical evil. (p. 22)

Two elements stand out in this passage.

First, Margalit uses the phrase "radical evil." He defines it, carefully; he does not see it often in the world, but he accepts that it can rear its ugly head and needs to be unabashedly branded. For many trained (as he and I both were) precisely in response to Hitler's actions and words, there may still be something shocking about the usage, even as applied to Hitler (you don't find the phrase in Gutmann and Thompson, who specifically resist Margalit in several passages, preferring the phrase "lesser evil" to justify outcomes such as the Constitutional Convention's "slavery compromise," of which more soon). There is a sense among such notable deconstructionists as Geoffrey Hartman, himself a survivor of Hitler's Berlin and my teacher in graduate school at Cornell and Zurich, that we can ethically respond to Hitler's grotesque rhetoric of racial prejudice only by *avoiding* such words, by indeed avoiding an absolutist rhetoric of *any kind*. I have disagreed with him,[8] finding as a central spur to this very volume that Europe caved not because of uncompromisingly grotesque rhetoric but because decent people and relatively good institutions failed to name *bluntly* what was good and bad in their midst. We should not let Hitler, in other words, discourage us from calling the world as it sometimes is, in shades of good and bad. Thus Margalit's willingness to utter the phrase "radical evil" situates him among those whose response to Hitler includes a willingness and even an obligation to name, uncompromisingly, what needs to be defended or undermined.

Second, as to compromise itself, an admission that there is "radical evil" in the world signifies a rigid, nonnegotiable barrier to compromise under certain, fortunately rare, conditions. The duty rests with each of us to figure out which situations (seldom, but sometimes) and which people (few and far between) create such a barrier.

We have here a very different "mindset" from the one propounded by Gutmann and Thompson.

Margalit, if he had stopped at this point, would have made a contribution to thinking on flexibility, because he welcomes a moral level of judgment and appeals to each reader's responsibility to be intractable in certain rare situations and regarding certain extremely bad potential negotiating partners. But he goes further and attempts to offer a taxonomy of "rotten compromises," ones that should be or should have been avoided.

> I see a rotten political compromise as an agreement to establish or maintain an inhuman regime, a regime of cruelty and humiliation, that is, a regime that does not treat humans as humans. (p. 2)

With some other conditions also met, this approach would have led Margalit's ideal reader to have rejected the original US Constitution once the convention in Philadelphia permitted slavery to endure in a way that inflicted humiliation on people for decades thereafter. An agreement, even reaping a benefit such as the founding of an otherwise reasonably decent republic, or in the context of pre-World War II Europe a potential lasting peace, is "rotten" when those subject to it but powerless to raise their voices against it are about to suffer from cruel treatment up to and including "crimes against humanity" (p. 67).

Unsurprisingly, the move made by Margalit toward "rotten compromise avoidance" is open to criticism, and not surprisingly, Gutmann and Thomson throw some brickbats at him. For example, Margalit chooses a period of time beyond which no amount of compromised human suffering is acceptable, and some readers may find this delineation somewhat arbitrary. But the main point, again, is one of vastly different perspectives on compromise and change, exemplified best by Gutmann and Thompson's take on the slavery deal hashed out in Philadelphia:

> Most historians agree that the unequal representation in the Senate [another major compromise at the founding] was probably necessary to secure ratification, but even here there is disagreement about exactly why the concession was needed. The historical judgment of the slavery compromise is still more complex.... The point is not to reach a conclusive verdict on whether this compromise was defensible but rather to suggest that assessments of major political compromises, even on the seemingly objective question of whether they were necessary and with all the advantages of hindsight, do not yield definitive yes or no judgments. (pp. 56–57)

The stark difference between these two books consists in Margalit's willingness to make judgments, to try to give us criteria, substance, a real-world view of how human beings operate. I learn from such an approach, even if I do not always share it— his philosopher's minutiae can stymie my more literary and legal thinking—because mature reflection on crucial issues legitimates what the always compromising and compromised Gutmann and Thompson resist on principle: "a conclusive verdict" and "yes or no judgments."

I join Margalit, too, in recognizing that traditions of religious discourse increasingly affect our view of compromise, for example, by establishing certain nonnegotiable "taboos"—"Even the tiniest piece of A should not be exchanged for the biggest amount of B" (p. 29). We need not be fundamentalists in the usual pejorative sense to feel occasionally the pushing back, provided by every moral tradition, on constant "change." What makes the book you are reading somewhat different, of course, is that I am arguing that *flexibility itself* originated in the deepest structures of early Christianity! So religion giveth excess flexibility as it taketh away freedom of choice in some domains. As we have seen, the fairly typical twenty-first-century liberal perspective of Gutmann and Thompson shows how deeply repugnant, how "taboolike," is the whole idea of "tenacity" in many quarters.

Flexibility has become a dogma, sometimes indistinguishable in its binding quality and the sanctions imposed on "unbelievers," from sacred religious commands.

Margalit's book, finally, shows how quickly policies we might abhor as a nation become acceptable, become "non-taboos," when we feel threatened. And this is of course precisely what happened in the early Jesus movement, when Paul conjured the end of days to propound a brilliant but distorted and ultimately cruel reading of the Jewish sacred texts. *Contemporary* emergency discourse has served under administrations led by blue-staters as well as red-staters to justify torture and "torture plus" after 9/11. Margalit puts it this way:

> We encounter the public sentiment telling the government "not in our name" when a government, supposed to represent us, does immoral things that it should not do. [This] happens when "we the people" are not in danger. In such circumstances, we can afford to be moral... .
>
> But when facing a significant adverse prospect that we perceive as a threat to our very lives, "we the people" have very little patience with claims about right and wrong, irrespective of their outcomes. In such cases ethical tribalism runs deeper than morality. (pp. 124–25)

What a boon to thoughtfulness we find here! Our pragmatic national compromise with post-9/11 distortions is a form of "tribalism" at best. But for Margalit the maximum dispensation after the fact—because each "emergency" always resolves, leaving us embarrassed about what "we the people" had wrought—

> is room for forgiveness or at least understanding, depending on the consequences of such a compromise. (p. 127)

3. Robert Mnookin's Mr. Spock

Robert Mnookin, like Avishai Margalit, examines many historical moments of choice between compromise and firmness. His book *Bargaining with the Devil* lies between the two works so far discussed because, like Margalit, he accepts the possibility of encountering evil but, like Gutmann and Thompson, he much prefers a baseline of compromise and a distaste for "gut reactions" as he calls them that might induce stubbornness instead of "rational" deliberation. His book also extends the treatment of negotiation to everyday, more personal struggles. Recognizing that the word "evil" is out of fashion and raises eyebrows, as I have signaled in admiring Margalit's unabashed willingness to use it, he reminds us that we often tend to see "evil" in many banal situations such as that of people getting divorced or renegotiating a contract or dealing with business partners by whom they feel they have been betrayed. He is right, of course, to remind his readers that almost any negotiating posture taken by "the other side" can inspire thoughts of "evil" that should be challenged before they become bars to resolving everyday conflicts. In all situations, big and small, Mnookin's test is, *Did you think it through?* (p. 104, italics in original).

And there's the rub, as Shakespeare's highly relevant Prince of Denmark put it. For Mnookin, nothing else matters in judging uncompromising behavior such as Churchill's in World War II, no saving grace except cogitation, even when we have the benefit of 20–20 hindsight showing how sound Churchill's intuitions proved to be. Until Mnookin determines that Churchill was just like us, that he "slept on it" before accepting what a lifetime of preparation and insight inspired in him, that he became like Prince Hamlet and insisted on delay when his fate and that of the world was "crying out"—until, in other words, Churchill *thought Hitler through*—he stands condemned.

Mnookin's insistence on weighing everything out cerebrally makes for good academic discussion but poor leadership. He ultimately commends Churchill solely because there is some historical evidence proving that the wartime prime minister, although "motivated by his personal moral beliefs and gut feelings," took a few days and "thought things through" (p. 103) before rejecting compromise.

I breathed a sigh of relief: Robert Mnookin, after much reflection and many pages, approves of Winston Churchill's impetuosity toward his wartime enemies!

Mnookin's analysis falls under the sign of Shakespeare's immortal play, *Hamlet*. I have long surmised that Churchill and Chamberlain (both discussed by Mnookin as they were by Margalit) had two different interpretations of the play. Prince Hamlet was faced with a decision about whether to eradicate "evil" or to allow an extensive rational process to emerge that both delayed action and cast into question the very notion of "evil." This is what makes Hamlet such a "modern" character: he avoids a knee-jerk leap into revenge and subjects his "gut" to constant thinking and rethinking. So, for Mnookin pondering Churchill, the unwillingness to compromise only becomes acceptable because Churchill-as-Hamlet seems to have "thought" for a while instead of simply following his mature, ingrained, and inflexible moral intuition. Chamberlain, in my imagination, was one of those admirers of Hamlet who always "quartered" his thinking—as the Prince puts it self-critically; no pure thought can lead to action. Every impulse must be reduced, parsed, compromised.

At what stage of our own maturation process have we finally experienced enough in the world to know what it takes to act rightly and to decline when much is at stake the temptation to reopen moral stances we long ago fixed for ourselves? This is the Churchill who first scolded Chamberlain at Munich for giving up Czechoslovakia for a spurious specter of "peace in our time" and who a bit later refused to negotiate a separate peace with the Fascists after the fall of France. Both prime ministers had read *Hamlet*. Churchill found in it a guideline for life: it is error to delay unduly (*some* thought is always necessary) when everything within you knows what is right. The Chamberlain who went into the Munich negotiations with Hitler over the fate of Czechoslovakia had read the play, too, but for him it meant that everything, always, was open to endless thinking and possible change, while for Churchill, some Rubicons had been crossed, their lessons learned, and their relevance to the present dilemma obvious.

It is too easy, and too fashionable, to judge a leader's "gut" action according to the latest blunder that hindsight allows us to criticize. We correctly set up George W. Bush's ill-advised invasion of Iraq, and this is arguably fair once we assume that Bush acted from the gut; he might have been the puppet of Dick Cheney or acting out subconsciously a Freudian urge to avenge his father's failure to bring down Saddam Hussein. But we need to reject, by recalling Churchill and MLK, any conclusion that one person's intuitive blunder forever indicts all actions by other mature individuals who rely mostly on their trained intuition and not on the infinite back and forth of cost-benefit pragmatic thinking.

The approach taken in *Bargaining with the Devil* somehow diminishes for a twenty-first-century reader some of the great twentieth-century models of behavior to which all might otherwise aspire. I began to yearn for Salman Rushdie's recent call for "courage of the life of the mind or of public figures," noted in Chapter 1. So I guess I would rather summon Mnookin as the fine mediator he is on the smaller, personal issues than as a tactician of great leadership or moral action in times of crisis.

Mnookin has immeasurably aided the flow of my own narrative, nonetheless, by introducing a personification of his baseline perspective. He recycles the ultimately rational Mr. Spock from *Star Trek* and inserts him in any situation where his reader might otherwise respond from the gut. Spock appears early and often. For example, he checks the rising fury of a businessman who feels he has been utterly betrayed by his partner and hence does not wish even to discuss with him what might be a useful new contract:

> Fortunately, you have a trusted advisor named Mr. Spock [who] is a clear thinker and a brilliant strategist. But he's not warm and fuzzy. He is emotionally detached, humorless,

someone your wife describes as a "cold fish."..."Let's keep the emotions out of it," Spock intones. Many of his conversations begin like this. (p. 22)

With Spock around, you never go with your intuition, no matter how mature and advanced it is. Cost-benefit analysis rules. Reason prevails, but of course it is only one way of understanding reason, a pragmatic, endless process of weighing situations, negotiating them, compromising them. Spock is the epitome of what Herman Melville, a lifelong skeptic about our compromising ways of understanding things, called an "intricate game of chess where few moves are made in straight-forwardness and ends are attained by indirection, an oblique, tedious, barren game hardly worth that poor candle burnt out in playing it."[9] Against that bleak assessment of the Spock-ian compromiser, Churchill's brand of behavior appears just as "reasonable," as influenced as it was by his trained emotional side, but even he might have bargained with Hitler and the Axis if Spock had been present to deflect his righteous energies.

4. A "Flexiphobe" in Lieu of a Mr. Spock

My version of Mnookin's Mr. Spock's coolly "pragmatic" cost-benefit analysis for any conceivable situation that challenges our sense of right and wrong is a trait I call "flexiphobia" and a carrier of that trait I admiringly label a "flexiphobe." Harnessing her life's experiences and trained intuition, the flexiphobe will occasionally insist on making judgments that do not open up the pragmatic door that has so often led to catastrophe. A very recent example is her response to the government's eavesdropping policies; for most people, a "debate" has begun about the details of something the flexiphobe knows should not become open to the equivocation that inevitably follows from intricate discussion.

In sticking to her judgment that the massive eavesdropping on citizens is wrong, the flexiphobe relies on a lifetime of experience and thought. She responds almost fearfully when advised to "go with the flow," the excitement others fatefully feel when "new" issues roil them. Her fear—her legitimate phobia toward excessive flexibility—is a sound one, akin to knowing in advance what happens when you put your hand into a roaring fire; she has read about Sully Sullenberger and knows that rational fear can be redirected toward positive outcomes.[10] Her absolutes, and there are not many of them but they are precious to her, survive the fearful world of constant equivocation.

Such absolutes are usually no more than what all three of the books just discussed might call "core values." She goes a step further, however, than privileging these values and yet permitting them to yield to exigent circumstances. She adopts positively what Gutmann and Thompson largely deride as "an uncompromising mindset," which once engaged on crucial issues refuses out of "principled tenacity" to compromise baseline tenets.

For the flexiphobe, the status quo occasionally requires unyielding preservation. Her antennae rise especially when others use the word "emergency" to unsettle previously sound traditions. After 9/11, for example, she held firm to 9/10's American constitutional values such as an opposition to torture or prolonged detention in places such as Guantanamo,[11] taboos that many of her colleagues were already negotiating out of existence on 9/12. Flexiphobes and their acolytes offend against many compromise writers' own baseline, which holds that preserving the status quo is *never* a good if a proposed negotiation of what exists—say, the taboo on torture—moves things toward a present perception of anything marginally different, say, adding a weapon to the war on terrorism.

Flexiphobes of this liberal stripe have studied and also lived through moments of crisis and apparently permanent change, through so-called states of exception, that is, "deviations from law and tradition encouraged by an 'emergency.'"[12] These tend to prove that, more often than not, the right response was taken by those very few individuals who declined to compromise and who insisted that a healthy status quo should be fought for and preserved instead of parsed and, often tragically if only temporarily, discarded.

Elaine Scarry's *Thinking in an Emergency,*[13] among other such studies, stands in opposition to the more mainstream imposition of, and tolerance for, limitless recalibrations of previously cherished norms. Scarry describes in great detail patterns of thought and behavior that permit people trained in crisis management to respond with habituated actions and words that protect most of the rest of us who have not done such work, who have little to offer to ourselves and others during emergencies. What neuroscientists call the amygdala, a kind of "personal alarm system" in the brain, starts to sound in such people, but instead of leading to flight from training and principle, the alarm sounds for their preservation. Compromise to the flexiphobe at times like this (and they are fortunately rare) has become as threatening to her well-being as others might find a dangerous animal in the forest or a seductive dessert in a restaurant.[14]

Working to keep alive a counter-flow response of intractability, such people substitute for limitless openness to the "new" a mature use of their "advanced intuition." Both words in that phrase are key. They involve a bit of what we colloquially call the "gut"—but it is how that instinct has been nurtured *experientially* that counts. Indeed, the phrase is best described and utilized in a field perhaps most connected to reason and deliberation: its guru is one of our greatest judges, Benjamin Nathan Cardozo. In various extra-judicial essays, Cardozo speaks of finding the right answer to a complex judicial problem not only through analytical logic but also through "flashes of insight" derived from "experience usually extensive and often profound."[15] In a famous 1932 speech to the New York State Bar Association, he speaks of the "hunch"—a more fruitful word than the "gut"—a "vivid and arresting description of one of the stages in the art of thought. The hunch is the divination of the scientist, the luminous hypothesis, the apocalyptic insight, that is back of his experiments."[16]

He quotes a renowned Rockefeller Institute professor, Dr. Alfred E. Cohn, who writes, "Intuition in this sense is speed applied to experience...[and] advanced intuition denotes the complex process I have been describing in which attention, perception, memory and extra-conscious ratiocination are involved." In Cardozo's essay, a great logical positivist joins forces with this view of the combined force in difficult choice situations of innate almost fixed experience and bursts of insight; so, Bertrand Russell:

I have found that if I have to write upon some rather difficult topic, the best plan is to think about it with very great intensity—the greatest intensity of which I am capable—for a few hours or days and at the end of that time give orders, so to speak, that the work is to proceed underground (i.e. subconsciously). After some months I return consciously to the topic and find that the work has been done. Before I had discovered this technique, I used to spend the intervening months worrying because I was making no progress; I arrived at the solution none the sooner for this worry, and the intervening months were wasted, whereas now I can devote them to other pursuits.[17]

The rare combination of faith in prior reasoning and fear of current equivocation leads to insights that in some way answer best the risk of "too much analysis," a risk that is as modern as the internet and cable TV and as old as Prince Hamlet and the men who compromised through interpretive distortion the Jewish sacred texts their cleverness changed into something "new." We turn now to the latter, as fascinating an example as can be found of limitless compromise and enduring flexiphobic resistance to it.

Notes

1. For a reminder of the different voices, many of them "red-staters," that counseled maintaining our policy against torture and other extreme techniques of interrogation and that led in 2005 to the Detainee Treatment Act, see Chapter 6, note 61.

2. See, e.g., "Brennan Faces Hurdles in CIA Interrogations," *New York Times*, March 7, 2013, p. A1 and p. A18: "The day after the Senate committee approved Mr. Brennan's nomination in a bi-partisan 12–3 vote, Senator Rand Paul, Republican of Kentucky, joined by a handful of other senators, carried out a filibuster on the nomination, protesting the Obama administration's refusal to rule out drone strikes on American soil in an emergency." See also the PBS version of the story at http://www.pbs.org/newshour/rundown/2013/03/paul-launches-filibuster-strike-against-administrations-drone-policy.html. It was only some days after the confirmation that the stalwart liberal and Armed Forces Committee Chair Carl Levin remarked on C-Span: "I had trouble with Brennan because he would not acknowledge that water-boarding was torture." March 18, 2013. See this book, chapter 6, note 75.

3. Why have Democrats, so long the Senate majority party, failed to fight out and win the annual battle on the filibuster? Why, in the terms of this book, are they always so flexible, so accommodating? Only as we near print—on Friday, November 22, 2013—have Senate Democrats made a modest move to check the Republican abuse of the filibuster; *New York Times*, November 22, 2013, p. A1.

4. See on the subject, Stephen L. Carter, "Evolutionism, Creationism, and Treating Religion as a Hobby," *Duke Law Journal* (1987): 977–94; and for a perspective sympathetic to religious beliefs in the context of First Amendment issues more generally, Michael M. McConnell,

"Accommodation of Religion," *Supreme Court Review* (1985): 1–23.

5. *DC v. Heller*, discussed further in Chapter 6.

6. The Democrats managed only to get an "up/down" vote on gun control in April, 2013, *not* to win.

7. Barry Goldwater Acceptance Speech, Republican National Convention, San Francisco, July 16, 1964.

8. See my elaborated response to this sustained component of Professor Hartman's writings in Weisberg, "Law and Literature as Survivor," in Austin Sarat et al., eds., *Teaching Law and Literature* (New York: Modern Language Association, 2011).

9. Herman Melville, *Billy Budd, Sailor,* ed. Harrison Hayford and Merton M. Sealts (Chicago: University of Chicago Press, 1962), pp. 86–87.

10. See discussion in Chapter 1, notes 1, 3, and 4.

11. The *New York Times* recently reported, "Polls show that Americans are increasingly indifferent to the prison" (April 26, 2013, p. A30), having already reported on April 7 that 65 percent of us "approve" of drone strikes. Equivocation on these issues by leading voices in academia and the media (including films and TV shows) leads to a "toughening" against anyone who might be a terrorist or is just hanging out with one, and for a while the original sound traditions against such practices are shelved. The cyclical return to the good, or so history teaches, is virtually guaranteed: renewed concern in the face of the torturing, force-feeding, and killing of people who may well be completely innocent eventually will bring about a restoration of the original taboos. See the extended discussion in Chapter 6, b., including notes 61–67.

12. A recent classic on states of emergency and exception is Giorgio Agamben, *State of Exception* (English transl.: 2003). See also my discussion of Nazi jurisprudential guru Carl Schmitt, whom Agamben cites frequently, in Chapter 4.

13. See Elaine Scarry, *Thinking in an Emergency*, ch. 1, notes. 1, 4.

14. For the physiology and neurology of these fear sensitive parts of our brain, see Gallwey, Hanzelik, and Horton, *The Inner Game of Stress*, ch. 1, n. 3: "the amygdala joins with the hypothalamus, the pituitary, and the adrenal glands to coordinate our most basic fight-flight-freeze responses to protect us from harm. The amygdala is activated automatically,

without thought," pp. 51–52. The flexiphobe fears flexibility, and the triggering mechanism is automatic in her; practice and thought, however, teach her not to freeze or flee in its presence.

15. See Benjamin N. Cardozo, *The Growth of the Law* (1924), p. 89; see also Margaret Hall, ed., *Selected Writings of Benjamin Nathan Cardozo* (New York: Bender, 1947), "NY State Bar Address" (1932), pp. 26–27.

16. Ibid., p. 28.

17. Ibid.

3

The Use and Abuse of Flexible Distortion in the New Testament and Early Christian Thought

a. Institutionalizing Excess Malleability by Damning the Steadfast: The Early Jesus Movement

Although training and decades of practice attune me reasonably well to a grasp of textual meanings—especially in law and literature—I realize as have others undertaking similar projects that the Bible is vast and complicated territory. I enter with enough modesty to have tried to sustain my analysis with readings from those who know more about the specific areas treated here, but I do not pretend to have mastery of even the complex hermeneutic questions I raise in this chapter. No one would make such a claim.

My emphasis follows from pioneers in the fields of literature and philology, not necessarily theology. My mentors are Friedrich Nietzsche (the careful philologist rather than the wild reader some have wrongly found him to be), Frank Kermode, Harold Bloom, James Carroll, and the Yale theologian Wayne Meeks, whose recent lecture on the fourth Gospel greatly inspired me.

My grasp of meanings in the Jewish biblical stories does benefit from some background in Hebrew and in Jewish ethics and law, and I have studied Talmud on occasion, but I am less adept still in the mysteries of what is called the "New Testament." Yet

I am content that the brilliant writers who ushered Christianity into the world wanted in the long run to attack those who rejected their message by labeling them "liars" and "rigid" and "blind," and that those labels institutionalized flexibility and made steadfastness into a diabolical rather than a positive trait.

The attack on inflexibility as a Jewish quality was not at first anti-semitic, because those leveling the charge were usually Jews themselves, and they lacked any trace of the overt racism that later characterized a segment of anti-semitic animus. Indeed, one pejorative they used—"stiff-necked"—came from the Five Books of Moses, though their emphasis was quite different. However, the consistent tone of these writers' repulsion in the face of Jewish steadfastness led eventually to that part of anti-semitism characteristic of Western Europe throughout the centuries and tragically culminating in the Holocaust; I have called this seemingly more rational variety of anti-Jewishness "anti-Talmudism."

There is a direct line between the Gospel writer John's portrait of unyielding Jewish loyalty to previously received traditions of meaning and morality and the conclusion reached in that text by Jesus himself (as so reported) that those Jews who resisted his messianic message were the sons of "the devil."[1] Such Jews are represented as bickering with Jesus and others, as hell-bent on totally undermining the beauty of Jesus's miracles, all because they cannot see beyond their strict laws and enduring textual traditions. As in the following passage, even their belief in One God and in Abraham as a patriarch who instituted monotheism is cast not only into question but into the pit of diabolical mendacity. Whether or not the following conversation (and many reported in John that are just like it) ever occurred, it etches into stone the counter-intuitive idea that merely sticking to what you believe is a morally bad thing:

John 8:52: The Jews said to him . . . 53. "Are you greater than our Father Abraham, who died? The prophets also died. Who do you claim to be?" 54. Jesus answered, "If I glorify myself, my glory is nothing. It is my father who glorifies me, he of whom you say 'He is our God,' though you do not know him. But I know him; if I would say that I do not know him, I would be a liar like you."[2]

History has been affected not only by the direct charge of deicide brought forward in such passages as Matthew 27:15–27;[3] my argument here is that the textual flexibility mandated to prove the messianic claim quickly required an equal and opposite lashing out at those committed to preserving with some faithfulness their own centuries-old traditions. Flexibility as a value sustains the Gospel according to John; those unwilling to go with the flow are pilloried by a narrative that everywhere exhibits a detestation of steadfastness.

1. Origins (and Origen's) Finding of Unlikely Meanings

In the early years of the Jesus movement, powerful writers codified, with seeming permanence, the project of limitless flexibility. Their target was the far less malleable, although still highly creative, system of Jewish religious understandings. In propounding the then new idea of the divinity of Jesus, men such as the brilliant St. Paul, formerly Saul of Tarsus, embarked on an almost impossible project: they felt the need to embed the Jesus idea in a set of Jewish sacred texts that meant something different from and often diametrically opposed to their new story. The Torah, the Prophets, and the Sayings would be ransacked with the aim of finding in them the presaging of Jesus-as-Messiah. As the philosopher Friedrich Nietzsche (the son of a Lutheran minister) described their task some centuries later:

> However much the Jewish scholars protested, everywhere in the Old Testament there were supposed to be references

to Christ and only to Christ and particularly his cross. Wherever any piece of wood, a switch, a ladder, a twig, a tree, a willow, or a staff is mentioned, this was supposed to indicate a prophecy of the wood of the cross; even the erection of the one-horned beast and the brazen serpent, even Moses spreading his arms in prayer, even the spits on which the Passover lamb was roasted—all are allusions to the cross and as it were preludes to it! Has anyone who asserted this ever believed it?...[But] they were conducting a war and paid more heed to their opponents than to the need to stay honest.[4]

As David Klinghoffer puts it more recently and less colorfully:

The Jews kept on guard against departures from inherited truths.[5]

The project of enlisting the entire Jewish Bible into the battle to prove the divinity of Jesus, or even that he was the Messiah, would have daunted lesser men than Paul for many reasons; two salient obstacles that became quite significant were, first, that the Jewish texts had been in place for more than eight centuries in some cases and had inspired a set of interpretations that gained respect and semi-permanence, at least regarding nonnegotiable issues such as the absolute unity of God and hardly more negotiable issues as what the Messiah would probably look like and the amazing feats he would accomplish when he finally showed up on earth. Second, these texts— in this respect and as we shall see in others as well, akin to the US Constitution—were *written*. Their enduring nature differed from what happened later in fixing the eventual New Testament canon. They remained in place with only minor emendations; as Bart D. Ehrman, who estimates the number of changes in New Testament narratives as being in the "thousands," says of the more stable Jewish textual tradition:

> Judaism was unique in that it stressed its ancestral traditions, customs, and laws, and maintained that these had been recorded in sacred books [that included] the laws that God gave Moses indicating how his people were to worship him and behave toward one another in community together, These were sacred laws, to be learned, discussed, and followed—and they were written in a set of books.[6]

2. Typology, Allegory, Foreshadowing, and *Presto! Everything Is New*

To fathom the challenge facing the early Christian movement, think about taking your favorite bedtime stories and upsetting them totally. You have understood "Hansel and Gretel" or "Goldilocks" a certain way, and then all of a sudden you are told that the wicked witch is the heroine, that Hansel and Gretel represent evil, and that the Three Bears are stand-ins for the Marx Brothers. Nothing stops these distortions from being offered, but you recognize them as satiric at best, weird at worst. You do not change your view of your favorite stories.

As Joroslav Pelikan reports in a largely sympathetic and wholly accessible account of Paul, John, and the first few centuries of Christianity's "stupendous claim,"[7] the work of overturning Jewish textual traditions was staggeringly more difficult than would be my task of convincing you that the Wizard of Oz was a high-tech genius comparable to Bill Gates. These brilliant first through third century conjurers proposed that every major figure and event in the Jewish Bible foreshadowed the coming of Jesus, and that the Jewish scriptures—whatever they seemed to mean in plain Hebrew[8]—now had been magically "fulfilled" in the coming of

Jesus. Pelikan identifies their transformative techniques as including "typology" and "foreshadowing" ("Christ was the second Adam…Mary the Second Eve)…part of an elaborate scheme of interpretation by which the liturgy prescribed in the Torah, especially Exodus and Leviticus, was seen as having become obsolete") (p. 96). "Prophecy and fulfillment" involved going beyond the Torah to the Prophets (especially Isaiah) and the Writings (especially the Psalms) and claiming that these "applied above all to the life, death, and resurrection of Jesus Christ" (p. 96).

Allegory may well be the most important means of transformation of meanings from "Old" to new traditions. Derived especially from Plato and perfected in its Christian form by the third-century writer Origen, allegory and its effects on Jewish texts are described by the post-Holocaust Protestant thinker, Franklin Littell:

> The Jewish Scriptures—selected portions of which were later to be designated "the Old Testament" in the Christian canon—were accorded respect through an allegorical exegesis which brings out the Christian and "spiritual" meanings but suppresses the historical and literal. Thus the uniqueness of events in specifically Jewish history is sacrificed.[9]

Early Christianity found a way to upset the Jewish texts' physical and moral meanings by finding hidden hints of Christ within them. The methods themselves are hardly foreign to Jewish as well as literary hermeneutics—after all, Paul *was* a Jew—and have had a minority of admirers among Jews, including very recently Daniel Boyarin, who cites Origen both as to his general method and a specific application:

> All the things in the visible category can be related to the invisible, the corporeal to the incorporeal, and the manifest

to those that are hidden.... [It] undoubtedly follows that the visible hart and roe mentioned in the *Song of Songs* are related to some patterns of incorporeal realities, in accordance with the character borne by their bodily nature. And this must be in such wise that we ought to be able to furnish a fitting interpretation of what is said about the Lord perfecting the harts, by reference to those harts that are unseen and hidden.[10]

Seen versus unseen; tangible versus hidden; accessible meanings versus obscure renderings: eventually, after all kinds of struggles and political transformations best described by James Carroll,[11] what seemed bizarre came into full authoritative control. Much may have been lost, however, in the process. Destabilization has its costs, and most Jewish interpreters, no matter how imaginative, quickly understood how the Christian reading methods trespassed on verisimilitude and even law:

Often, *midrash aggadah* [traditional Jewish interpretations of the Bible] is confused with allegory, which interprets a text according to its underlying or hidden meaning.... To the early Christian exegetes, allegory was a convenient way of accepting the sanctity of the Old Testament without being troubled by its content and laws. Unlike Midrash, allegory denies the plain meaning of the text.... The literal meaning is removed, revealing something altogether different. Maimonides emphasizes this point most clearly.[12]

3. The Focus on *Isaiah*

Now the textual basis for Jesus-as-Messiah is usually given as a compendium of allegedly prophetic verses in such Hebrew texts as Isaiah 52–53 or Psalms (e.g., 69:8,9); both of these are evoked in John. Yet any reader of these and other commandeered texts must grapple with the long tradition of understanding—still (frustratingly?) adhered to by Jewish exegetes, and by many modern Christian readers—that denies any plausible stretch from these Jewish texts to someone like Jesus-as-Messiah, however admirable he otherwise was. Perhaps the most famous application of all three methods is the misreading that makes out some chapters in Isaiah to be a prefiguring of Jesus-as-Messiah.

I am going to cite some of these verses, using a standard Hebrew-English edition. They are estimated to have been written in the eighth century BCE, around the time of Homer.[13] But while the gods in the *Iliad* were never thought to "prefigure," as though intentionally, any forthcoming religion, Isaiah's words were going to be used exactly that way, and by a group of learned readers deliberately departing from excellent, established patterns of meaning and even of monotheism. As would be true of most Jewish citations to a biblical text, the edition and translation I am using here have little in common with the King James or any other authoritative Christian version; I am assisted a bit by some familiarity with the original Hebrew, which I interpolate only once here to show the reader a translation variant at the most familiar line in the passage:

Behold, My servant shall prosper,
He shall be exalted and lifted up, and shall be very high (Isaiah
*   52: 13)...*
Who would have believed our report?
And to whom hath the arm of the Lord been revealed?
For he shot up right forth as a sapling,
And as a root out of a dry ground;
He had no form nor comeliness that we should look upon him,
Nor beauty that we should delight in him.

He was despised, and forsaken of men,
A man of pains [or "sorrows": "eesh machovot"] and acquainted with
    disease ["v'iyduah choli"].
And as one from whom men hide their face:
He was despised, and we esteemed him not.
Surely our diseases he did bear, and our pains he carried;
Whereas we did esteem him stricken,
Smitten of God, and afflicted.
But he was wounded because of our transgressions,
He was crushed because of our iniquities:
The chastisement of our welfare was upon him,
And with his stripes we were healed. (53:1–5)[14]

Most secular readers will know some of this language from its central place in Handel's *Messiah*. The composer had sixteen or more centuries behind him during which Christians had associated all of these lines with Jesus. Analogously and extremely relevantly, the Jewish audience to Jesus and his disciples already had centuries of tradition behind them that held out no chance for the Jesus claims being embodied in Isaiah. So what is now an effortless association through music and flexible interpretation should be rendered problematic; what began with the Gospel writers may be a cyclical aberration that will one day be set "right" once again.

For the new readers, everything about "the servant" was supposed to be a prediction of Christ. To the common reader of the original text, even today, the link seems obscure, even dead wrong.

Thus, in a twentieth-century Jewish commentary on Isaiah 53:3 ("he was despised...") and the surrounding verses, the traditional understanding is espoused that Isaiah is rendering no single individual—past, present, or future; instead, the post-exile prophetic writer conjures the renewal of Israel, described with admiration for its ability to survive after so much suffering: "The Babylonians, or their representatives, having known the servant, i.e., exiled Israel idealized, in his humiliation and martyrdom, and now seeing his exaltation and new dignity, describe their impressions and feelings."[15] The internal voice of the text at this point, in other words, may be that of the Babylonians reporting sympathetically on contemporary Israel after the siege of the holy city. All of this is consistent with long-standing Jewish readings, which have survived—along with those of so many passages in the commandeered older texts—the radical changes of the flexible interpreters. The twentieth-century traditional commentator pauses—quite untypically—to "answer" the long-standing Christian mis-reading:

> The servant is the ideal Israel or the faithful remnant. That he is not an individual is the opinion of all Jewish and most modern non-Jewish commentators. "Whatever causes may have tended to stimulate the advocacy of this form of interpretation (viz. the Christological), it is important for Christian exegetes to recognize that this path of Jewish exposition is in the main right, and that the path of Christian interpreters down to the time of Rosenmueller (i.e. 1820) has been in the main wrong.[16]

In our own times, as the Jewish commentator notes, fewer Christians have insisted on the implausible Christological reading. But the extreme openness to new and unlikely meanings engendered by early Christian exegesis of the Hebrew Bible is still alive and well.

Whatever the final judgment of history and morality on the way Christianity has commandeered Jewish sacred texts for its own ends—Harold Bloom believes the jury is still out on that judgment[17]—two themes of my book stand out: first, the early

Jesus movement's readings required the ultimate in "flexibility" to derive Jesus-as-Messiah from characters, stories, and legal codes that seemed impervious to such a claim; and second, unlike other extremely pliable textual interpreters, these early Christian era writers lashed out violently at those who resisted their meanings, and from then on steadfastness got a very bad name indeed.

The Gospels themselves and related writings that came to be grouped as the "New Testament" present in bold terms as villains and moral degenerates those Jews who wished only to be left alone with their meaning-traditions, the equivalent of most folks' insistence that the tortoise and hare story comes out in favor of slowness and steadiness and not, through some flexible new reading, on the side of the hare.

b. St. Paul's Use of "Emergency"

When people become convinced they are in the midst of a substantial emergency, they often lose whatever respect they might have had for traditions such as textual accuracy or even the law. Paul believed that the world was coming to an end, the ultimate emergency that produced his "urgent talk," as A. N. Wilson puts it toward the end of an authoritative account of Paul's life and writings: no wonder Paul believed and codified that "righteousness was unattainable for the human race."[18] Fear as much as faith, perhaps, helped some of his audiences to accept the extreme malleability of his biblical interpretations. In Galatians, for example, Paul exhibits the new movement's methodology of using Jewish sacred texts to substantiate radical new positions, such as the claim that following the law no longer counts as long as one has faith.[19] The argument in Galatians does not always cite these older texts accurately—there are actual changes made to the Hebrew Bible when Paul quotes it—but more important, there are such gigantic interpretive leaps as to leave the Jewish community either gasping, or (much more prevalently) indifferent, in the face of such mis-readings!

> Galatians 3:6: Just as Abraham "believed God, and it was reckoned to him as righteousness," (Genesis 15:6) 7. So, you see, those who believe are the descendants of Abraham. 8. And the scripture, foreseeing that God would justify the Gentiles by faith, declared the gospel beforehand to Abraham, saying, "All the Gentiles shall be blessed in you." (Genesis 12:3; 18:18) 9. For this reason, those who believe are blessed with Abraham who believed. 10. For all who rely on the works of the law are under a curse, for it is written, "Cursed is everyone who does not observe and obey all the things written in the book [*sic*] of the law." (Deuteronomy 27:26)... 24. Therefore the law was our disciplinarian until Christ came, so that we might be justified by faith." (Levine and Brettler, p. 337)[20]

Galatians resonates with Paul's huge claim that faith, and not works-through-strict-law, is the road to salvation. Good enough, perhaps, the argument standing alone points to individualistic acceptance of God rather than communal obedience predicated on the far less flexible dictates of "the Book." The impassioned call forthrightly substitutes subjective faith for flexiphobic law, and it has had in and of itself enormous (perhaps predictable) appeal. I have been arguing, remember, that loyalty to established patterns such as obedience to God by following law, or many secular commitments not involving a deity, requires hard work. Faith is less stressful, perhaps, and gives us a good deal of wiggle room. Astonishing, however, is Paul's pervasive insistence on justifying this striking innovation by distorting older texts that rigorously resist such a theology. Why the need to manhandle, through excessively flexible textual interpretation, the established meaning of the Jewish verses in Genesis and Deuteronomy? (The overt misquotation from Deuteronomy is the Galatians' passage's least notable trespass upon the Mosaic texts!)[21] Why has it become necessary to take a figure like Abraham and transform him, fantastically, into a precursor of this new idea? Abraham, like most Jewish heroes, approached God through a mixture of faith and law. One cannot exist without the other, at least not in the older sacred texts Paul insisted on commandeering.

The "emergency" and the exigencies of the messianic claim seemed to require an ethos of maneuverability beyond all possible meanings plausibly derivable from the Jewish texts. Flexibility was on its way. It became a model, still used often, when authorities demand departures from previously held, soundly maintained, and sometimes sacred positions.

Crisis conditions, from Paul to the present post-9/11 environment, have demanded "new" and flexible thinking.

c. John's Unsteady "B-Plot"

The early Jesus movement's model applied and was perfected even—or really, *because*—there was no pressing emergency remaining except the movement's own needs. Later writers such as John had to deal, irksomely, with the reality of earthly life's banal continuation. As theologian Wayne Meeks puts it, "If the urgency of early Christianity's claims was posited on the expectation that the world was about to end, an event which did not occur, then the basis of Christian ethics seemed to be undermined." Meeks adds that, for this and other reasons, "The Christians had to prove that they were not the upstart superstition that traditionalist members of the society were bound to see in them. For both internal and external reasons, then, it was essential that they find ways to incorporate Israel's story into their own."[22]

The multiple tasks John may have set himself seem to have contributed to a narrative technique that is not always easy to grasp. Meeks, a theologian to be admired and respected, has also very recently called this fourth Gospel "very weird" in the way it tells its story.[23] The primary conundrum that I want to focus on is the fact that the world around John was as bad a place as it ever had been, and that Jesus's presence here changed not one iota of that sad reality. The world went on through that turbulent Temple-destroying, rebellious first century: lions were not lying down with lambs, swords were not being melted into plowshares, and men were still learning war. Yet the reality check of the situation on the ground only seemed to embolden the original Pauline enterprise of proving the Jesus-as-Messiah claim through "off the wall" readings of such Jewish texts as Isaiah, Psalms, Genesis, and Deuteronomy.

Paul's eschatology having been disproved, we might say, his hermeneutics had to prevail. John, in particular, carried the ball. When the world neither ended nor improved, as the old texts said it must if there was a true Messiah at work, those texts not only needed to be manipulated flexibly but—more important still—the idea of textual fidelity had to be violently excoriated. No historical example is as important to my theme of the risks of excessive flexibility as this negation of textual and legal steadfastness.

By the time we get to the Gospel according to John, the paradox had created a second need that was almost as vital to the movement as the claim of Jesus's divinity. As many have agreed in discussions I report earlier in this chapter, the entire Jewish Bible was being contorted through readings that would formally fall under the rubrics "typology," "foreshadowing," and "allegory."

Some had accepted these readings and the messianic claim they underlay, but most had not.

So as John took up Paul's cudgels, he had to explain why the world continued, unimproved. He lashed out with a verbal violence rarely seen in the older texts, which Christianity has eventually tarred with the brush of "eye-for-an-eye" primitiveness, against the reluctant Jewish textualists. It just drives him over the edge to find that his co-religionists have failed to see "the light."

John's Gospel creates what we would now call a "B plot" to resolve his own anger by placing moral blame on the Jews for sticking to their own beliefs. Another way of stating this would be to see a two-front war in his Gospel. John continues the struggle to substantiate the Jesus-as-Messiah claim. There are touching descriptions of miracles, and you can find some uplifting sermons from the great teacher. But the second front, which the narrative technique shows to be just as important to him as the first, is to denigrate forever notions of fidelity to tradition. He etches in stone, through the B plot's often caricatured representations of Jews, a code that violently denigrates the whole idea of allegiance itself to prior traditions of law, text, and meaning. In a brutal climax, the Jews are called "devils" and made responsible for the crucifixion.

So John sets about to show, in his explosive narrative rendition of the Jews' "rejection" of Jesus, that the entire idea of fidelity to textual meaning was not only interpretively but also *morally* wrong! The logic worked this way: the Jewish Bible and Jewish law mandated with reasonable strictness a certain description of the Messiah and a definite happy ending upon his appearance; no such Messiah and certainly no such blissful culmination had taken place in Jesus; yet Jesus is the Messiah; therefore, strict allegiance to text and law is itself morally bankrupt. The logic leads to a conclusion that sets the moral and hermeneutic universe into a spin: the greater the departure from likely textual meaning, the more acceptable the interpretation, and the more the interpreter sticks to the text, the more reprehensible the practice and the more "false" the conclusion!

In John 7, one of many scenes in the B-plot finds Jews responding skeptically to the idea that Jesus might be the Messiah. They wonder (in verses 40–44), for example, about whether the Messiah was supposed to descend from David and come from Bethlehem. Their skepticism or indifference to the Jesus movement is overtly linked to their interpretive strategy of *sticking to the text*. But the narrative, having deliberately decided to introduce these Jewish objections, always paints them as nitpicking, legalistic, inflexible, and uncompromising.

St. John emphasizes the stubbornness of those resisting the new movement. If they stood impassive within their own reading traditions, John would attack the very methods that led them to feel somewhat secure about their sacred text's meanings. Not only must the textual understandings be distorted; *distortion as a hermeneutic principle must be ensconced and ratified.*

By peppering his account of miracles with examples of Jewish intrangisence, John furthers a process of change that eventually will reduce textual fidelity itself to a kind of unspiritual baseness. He really dislikes flexiphobes, and the breathtaking accounts of miracles somehow must show his resentment, no matter how astounding they would have been standing just on their own! A reader coming fresh to John's fifth chapter may admire in it passages such as this miracle of healing:

> John 5:1. After this there was a festival of the Jews, and Jesus went up to Jerusalem. 2. Now in Jerusalem by the Sheep Gate there is a pool...which has five porticoes. 3. In these lay many invalids, blind, lame, and paralyzed. [Jesus sees a man who had been lying there sick for thirty-eight

years.] . . . 8. Jesus said to him, "Stand up, take your mat, and walk." 9. At once the man was made well and he took up his mat and began to walk.

This is a beautiful story. But what follows is not:

. . . Now that day was a sabbath. 10. So the Jews said to the man who had been cured, "It is the Sabbath; it is not lawful for you to carry your mat." 11. But he answered them, "The man who made me well said to me 'Take up your mat and walk.'" [Later] 15. The man went away and told the Jews that it was Jesus who had made him well. 16. Therefore the Jews started persecuting Jesus, because he was doing such things on the sabbath. (Levine and Brettler, pp. 167–68)

So it is that St. John's two-front war makes the destruction of a certain flexiphobic interpretive approach seem as significant as his celebratory insistence on a messianic savior. As Frank Kermode has noted with a compelling mix of admiration and distaste, such B-plot accounts in the Gospels lend a kind of historical specificity to the seemingly more edifying miracle narratives.[24] The possibility that such mean-spirited responses never really occurred, or remained purely private, yields to the power of seeming to ground in at least some human reality what is of course otherwise a miracle story. But the upshot of the story's sideshow has made the B-plot more important over time than the central event. The old texts, with their reverence for law faithfully interpreted and practiced, are preserved at the significant cost of decimating a steadfast tradition of careful reading.

John 5:39. You search the scriptures, because you think that in them you have eternal life; and it is they that testify on my behalf. 40. Yet you refuse to come to me to have life 41. I do

not accept glory from human beings. 42. But I know that
you do not have the love of God in you. (Levine and Brettler,
p. 169)

In other words, Jews, if you decline to interpret your own texts
and your law with the extraordinary pliability needed by our new
account, you are very bad, do not deserve God's love, and will
never see salvation.

We are still living with this remarkable turn-about in perception, which began with terrifyingly original readings of Jewish
sacred texts. Although Jewish biblical interpreters prior to Paul
and John also performed brilliant leaps of textual understanding,
they always performed their interpretive feats flexiphobically,
that is, remaining in what biblical scholar Barry S. Kogan has recently described as "broadly acceptable limits."[25] Furthermore,
creative textual interpretations declined to stretch the boundaries beyond these limits; the wildest scans performed by Jews on
their own texts, Kogan tells us, traditionally had to do not with
relatively clear-cut predictions such as those dealing with the
Jewish Messianic tradition but rather with "unclear, implausible
or otherwise problematic [areas of] the received meanings and
mandates," regarding which "new interpretations consistent
with truth and goodness could eventually be found." Allegorical
understandings, for example, enrich Jewish interpretations of
the Bible; but allegory itself meets its limit case when it purports
to transform the law's plain meaning.

Interpretive creativity is a good thing, but when it comes to
the more precious of traditions and texts, wisdom and experience counsel caution and boundedness. Surely Talmudic discussions over the centuries include remarkable interpretive flights
of fancy, but there can be no doubt that some interpretations
(e.g., finding the Jesus story in the Book of Isaiah or, even more
outrageously, dividing the one God into a trinity)[26] are unacceptable

and will remain so against all external pressures to find them valid. Change is possible without total distortion, or in the words of Talmudic scholar Samuel Hoenig:

> A viable system of law must not sacrifice either its spirit or its letter. Hasty compromises, unfounded alterations, and whimsical abandonment of legal traditions lead only to chaos. In order for a legal system to endure and flourish, it is necessary for the law to be flexible, elastic, and fluid, as well as definitive, clear, and steadfast.[27]

John's tactics, building on Paul's, pushed those last three adjectives to the limit. No wonder that each generation since has wondered about and tried to fathom the interpretive strategies set in place so long ago. They have fascinated two millennia of readers, many of them admiring, some—particularly perhaps since the Holocaust—skeptical. Among superb recent readers of John, Harold Bloom speaks of the "violently anti-Jewish John" while also recognizing John as "a strong writer," because only such a storyteller could succeed in imposing so many misreadings (say, of Moses in the wilderness as somehow anticipating Jesus), which constituted "a plain lie against the text":

> I don't see how any authentic literary critic could judge John as anything better than a flawed revisionist of the Yahwist, and Paul as something less than that.... The central procedure of the New Testament is the conversion of the Hebrew Bible into the Old Testament, so as to abrogate any stigma of belatedness that might be assigned to the New Covenant, when contrasted with the "Old" Covenant.[28]

Kermode, on whom Bloom rightly relies, also recognizes the strength of John's narrative technique, which manages to produce verisimilitude through use of the ancient texts and other devices but still somehow provokes us to fear that John and others "lied.... We are aware that a particular view of the world, about what must or ought to happen, affects accounts of what does or did happen.... We should never underestimate our predisposition to believe whatever is presented under the guise of an authoritative report and is also consistent with the mythological structure of a society from which we derive comfort, and which it may be uncomfortable to dispute."[29] Kermode and Bloom both recognize that John and other Jesus movement pioneers caught onto something that went beyond aesthetics and even, perhaps, morality: they successfully appealed to the all-too-human preference for flexibility over steadfastness. But the turn to situational-based distortion as over and above a prior tradition of forthrightness had a ripple effect; as we will see in the next chapter, at least some of the disaster of Hitler's Europe can legitimately be ascribed to it.

Among Christian theologians, John and the other early writers have been the critical object of much commendable post-Holocaust commentary. Thoughtful Christians like Franklin Littell[30] anguish about the Gospel writers' more obviously anti-semitic verses: "Let his blood be upon us and our children" (Matthew 27:25) has wreaked havoc upon Jews down through the centuries. But with Kermode and Bloom, I am emphasizing something else, something more subtle and far more universal; something, indeed, that still affects fully secular and nonsuperstitious attitudes today. My claim has to do with these writers' general strategy of destroying less malleable modes of reading and understanding in order to achieve situational goals.

Between the first-century Gospel writers and the victory of their reading methods lay an increasingly powerful movement, which was able even during its first four centuries and up to the time of Augustine and Constantine, to institutionalize malleable misreadings; as Protestant theologian Littell summarizes it:

By the time of "The Teaching of the Twelve Apostles" (Didache, early second century), ill feelings towards "the hypocrites"—the Jews, professors of a false religion—are clearly evident....In the "Epistles" of Ignatius of Antioch (ca. 70–107), the de-Judaizing force of gentile Christian prejudice is also pronounced.... "The Epistle of Barnabas" probably dates from the first century, and until the fourth century it was included among the sacred books read out loud in Christian congregations. The writer...used the allegorical method of interpreting Scripture.... The author does not go so far as later gentile heretics like Marcion and most Gnostics, who cut the church from her Jewish heritage and denied the particularism and "materialism" of the Jewish Scriptures altogether.[31]

The powerful interweaving of law and narrative in the Jewish texts gave way to a series of new stories that questioned the value of the law and its flexiphobic interpreters. If Isaiah preached redemption through return to the law, his words could be woven into new stories that demoted law and privileged faith in Jesus, a figure flexibly adduced from the older text. But to admit John's understanding into such texts required more *textual flexibility* than the textual experts (or, I imagine, most reading communities dealing with familiar and precious stories) were willing to show. These were, after all, *sacred texts received not without creative variation but nonetheless within certain hermeneutic bounds* that were being stretched to fantastical limits by the intervening and—so the Christians hoped—"superseding" interpretation.

In bitterly portraying Jewish adherence to interpretive tradition as a kind of coldhearted legalism, Paul, John, and many of the other Jesus movement writers launched a worldview that systematically reduced law and text to a near secondary status unless the believer or reader adopted the "spiritual" stance newly required and associated uniquely with a private belief in the divinity of Jesus. Later authoritative Christian thinkers, perhaps especially St. Augustine, continued to preserve an idea of law but to associate it with something "lower" than the spiritual essence of the faith claims that superseded textual faithfulness. The distaste for strict readings is translated into a hierarchy of approaches privileging the nonmaterial, the figurative, we might almost say the "flexible":

> Nothing is more fittingly called the death of the soul than when that in it which raises it above the brutes, the intelligence namely, is put in subjection to the flesh by adhering to the letter.[32]

As Peter J. Tomson describes that fourth-century move: "Augustine also grasped the underlying problem [stated as follows by Franz Overbeck:] 'How could the Old Testament Law in its literal sense be suspended without encroaching upon the pre-Christian reverence for it which Christianity adopted along with the Old Testament itself?' Augustine's solution is a 'historization' of the abolition of the Law: although fundamentally the Law deserved respect it had become superfluous with the advent of Christ's gospel.... After Christ the commandments could in principle be observed 'without any necessity in view of salvation.'"[33]

Jews and their law gradually became linked with a "mere corporeality" (the body), while the Christians and their original textual deviations were elevated to the status of "spiritual" superiority. Opposed to the Letter, on this view, was the Spirit. This dualism is not only false as an organic metaphor that divides what are in fact dynamically integrated parts of the individual human corpus, but it also misunderstands the interrelationship of "strict Jewish law" to interpretive traditions that are *both* bounded (i.e., within limits) and interpretively open in their application to actual cases.[34]

Over the earliest Christian centuries, the elaborate system of laws established in the older "Testament" could be denigrated, and it was "replaced" or at least "fulfilled" by personal faith alone, and the commandment to "Love thy neighbor," values that of course the older text repetitively revered on its own. And what was to develop when Christianity attained secular power? The beautiful-sounding new spirit, deliberately uncoupled from the old system of well-understood ethics and law, struggled to work on earth. What would law—often so maligned in the sacred Christian texts—look like under Christian rulers? Would it become crueler, especially to outsiders, than the worst caricature of Jewish law itself?[35] Or might codes, like Magna Carta or post-Enlightenment constitutions, strive—often uneasily—to make the older idea of law again respectable?

Programmatic denigration of text, law, and interpretive tradition proved to be a mistake that has had repercussions far beyond the already fraught competition among religions. A world that had avoided the turn to excessive flexibility in dealing with others, with evidence, and with morals would have been a very different place indeed. I am not arguing it would have been to everyone's liking, or very easy to maintain as a dominant mode of behavior, but nonetheless intransigence deserved a better deal than that handed to it by tradition-breaking proselytizers and their secular emissaries beginning of course with Constantine's acceptance in the fourth century of Christianity as the dominant European religion.[36]

There follows in the next chapter an account of these brilliant early Christian writers' most tragic sequel.

Notes

1. The excellent text and translation of the New Testament that I use throughout is Amy-Jill Levine and Marc Z. Brettler, eds., *The Jewish*

Annotated New Testament (New York: Oxford University Press, 2011), here p. 176.

2. Ibid., pp. 176–77.

3. Ibid., p. 50.

4. Freidrich Nietzsche, *The Dawn of Day* (1881), Aph. # 84, transl. J. M. Kennedy (1924), in *The Complete Works of Freidrich Nietzsche*, edited by Oscar Levy (New York: Russell and Russell, 1964).

5. David Klinghoffer, *Why the Jews Rejected Jesus* (New York: Doubleday, 2005), p. 17. See also note 14, this chapter.

6. Bart D. Ehrman, *Misquoting Jesus* (San Francisco: HarperCollins, 2005), pp. 19–20.

7. Jaroslav Pelikan, *Whose Bible Is It?* (New York: Penguin, 2005), p. 90. Pelikan sets forth the *ways* in which the first several centuries of developing Christian reading techniques all tried to substantiate "the Christian belief, which is at work already throughout the New Testament and through most of subsequent Christian history, that by the authority of prophecy and fulfillment the Jewish Scripture was now Christian Scripture and had been meant to be this all along" (pp. 92–93). See also the seminal text on these various biblical and literary interpretive methods, Frank Kermode, *The Genesis of Secrecy* (Cambridge, MA: Harvard University Press, 1979), pp. 109, 113. Kermode treats, via Erich Auerbach, the Jesus movement's use of "typology"—the so-called fulfillment of Jewish Bible figures and events in the new story's narrative, p. 104 ff. In this way, everything in the older sacred text is grist for the mill of radical new meanings. See also Wayne A. Meeks, *The Origins of Christian Morality* (New Haven, CT: Yale University Press, 1993), pp. 207–10.

8. A fundamental set of difficulties of understanding arose just by virtue of the fact that the early Jesus movement and many verses in the New Testament itself relied on a Greek translation of the Jewish Bible called the Septuagint. For an excellent account of this problem of translation, see Levine and Brettler, *The Jewish Annotated New Testament*, at p. 159, n. 23 (a use of Isaiah) and p. 160, n. 50 (a use of Psalms) for two of many examples of mistranslations at key points in the Gospel of John, at 1:23 and 1:49; see also ibid., at p. 562 for an essay by Leonard Greenspoon on problems of understanding when working from the Septuagint, as opposed to the Hebrew Bible itself. See Pelikan, *Whose Bible Is It*, p. 65, where he surmises that "Some later Jews came to regret the translation of their Scriptures into Greek because of the Christian

usage of the Septuagint version of the Book of Isaiah to prove various doctrines such as the virgin birth of Jesus."

For a small list of translation problems that permitted Christians to find prefigurations of Jesus in the Five Books of Moses, see, e.g., J. H. Hertz, ed., *Pentateuch and Haftorahs*, 2d ed. (London: Soncino, 1960), p. 202.

9. Franklin Littell, *The Crucifixion of the Jews* (New York: Harper & Row, 1975), ch. 2, n.15, p. 27.

10. Daniel Boyarin, "Origen as Theorist of Allegory," in R. Copeland and P. T. Struck, eds., *Allegory* (Cambridge: Cambridge University Press, 2010), p. 40. Boyarin goes on to quote David Dawson on the passage from *Song of Songs*, finding that Origen speaks of "a visceral fluid present in the hart that improves eyesight and 'the vision that Christ both has and affords.'"

11. James Carroll, *Constantine's Sword* (Boston: Houghton Mifflin, 2001), this book, ch. 1, note 8.

12. Samuel N. Hoenig, *The Essence of Talmudic Law and Thought* (Northvale, NJ: Aronson, 1993), pp. 60–61. Maimonides and Rashi, among other authorities, cautioned against tipping the interpretive scales too much toward the figurative. Many Christians, of course, also privilege the literal.

13. Some of Isaiah was written later. *Isaiah*, Hebrew text and English translation; introduction and commentary by I. W. Slotki (London: Soncino, 1961). Slotki situates the authorship of this text to mid-eighth century BCE, around the time of the Syrian and Egyptian ravaging of Judah.

14. Using the original Hebrew helps to avoid the problems of translation through the Septuagint (see note 8), perhaps most acutely seen in (deliberate?) misperceptions of the Book of Isaiah. Klinghoffer (note 5) observes:

> What to do with Matthew's first explicit citation from a Hebrew prophet, Isaiah, with its doctrine of the virgin birth? This is a famous mistranslation: "Behold, a virgin [Greek, *parthenos*] shall conceive and bear a son, and his name shall be called Emmanuel." The "virgin" whom the Gospel has in mind, Mary, "had been betrothed to Joseph [but] before they came together she was found to be with child by the Holy Spirit." The writer was working from his text in the Greek scriptures, the Septuagint. However, the Hebrew original calls the lady in question not a "virgin," but merely a "young woman" (*almah*) who—as the word is used in Hebrew Scripture— could be married or single, sexually experienced or not. In Isaiah's words, there is no intimation of a virgin birth. If this prophecy was

ever cited in Jesus's lifetime, any biblically literate Jew would quickly have seen the problem. Parenthetically, one might also mention that Jesus's name was not "Emmanuel."...Pointing out the imprecision of proof texts like these, one feels almost unsporting. It's too easy. Yet it is with these that the New Testament begins its first attempt at a narration of the life of the Christian Messiah. Whoever the first educated Jews were to have these prophetic verses cited to them, whether in Jesus's lifetime or later, they could have reacted only with puzzlement and disbelief. (pp. 65–66)

15. Soncino edition of *Isaiah*, comment at p. 261.

16. Ibid., p. 260. See also Isaiah 9: 5-6 ("A child is born to us..."): "The reference is not to any future Messiah, nor to anyone yet unborn," Sonino edition, *Pentateuch and Haftorahs* (London, 1987). "Christian scholars of some repute are gradually giving up such partisan interpretations." Ibid., p. 202.

17. Harold Bloom, *Jesus and Yahweh* (New York: Penguin, 2005), this book, ch. 1, note 8: "Historically, both the New Testament and the Qur'an have pragmatically eclipsed the Hebrew Bible, but these successes are neither aesthetic nor necessarily spiritual, and Yahweh may not yet have spoken his final word upon this matter" (p. 37). See also this book, Chapter 6, note 52.

18. As James Carroll recounts Paul's eschatology, there was a far greater influence on him than fear of Roman oppression: "[P]erhaps a stronger determinant for Paul's theological preoccupation was his clear conviction that the End Time, with the return of Christ, was imminent." Carroll, *Constantine's Sword*, p. 139. And see A. N. Wilson, *Paul: The Mind of the Apostle* (New York: Random House, 1998), p. 154; "Paul believed, and the letter he had written [to the Romans] before arriving in Jerusalem makes it perfectly clear, that the messianic prophecies were to be fulfilled through himself and his fellow-Christians who shared a belief in 'his Gospel.' 'You know what time it is, how it is now the moment to wake up from sleep. For salvation is nearer to us now than when we became believers; the night is far gone, the day is near'" (p. 206). A tendency to "compromise" during emergencies began here and helps to explain Paul's need (and genial ability!) to deform the Jewish Bible to address the "crisis," which—like other self-styled "emergencies"—never ends.

19. As Bloom puts it, "[A]ll of the New Testament is obsessed with an anxious relationship to the Law and the Prophets, and seeks to resolve a complex anguish resulting from that overwhelming influence, by the

strongest and most successful creative misreading in all of textual history" (p. 36). The focal point of Paul's seeming antinomianism (distaste for the law) is his confrontation with Peter in Antioch, recounted in Galatians 2, 3. A nuanced discussion of these chapters and of Paul's view of the law generally is found in E. P. Sanders, *Paul, the Law, and the Jewish People* (Philadelphia: Fortress Press, 1983), e.g., ch 1: "The Law Is Not an Entrance Requirement." Despite the "plain meaning" of many of Galatians' verses, such as the following, not everyone sees Paul as a thoroughgoing hater of Mosaic law: "We ourselves, who are Jews by birth and not Gentile sinners, yet who know that a man is not justified by works of the law but through faith in Jesus Christ, even we have believed in Christ Jesus, in order to be justified by faith in Christ, and not by works of the law, because by works of the law shall no one be justified.... For all who rely on works of the law are under a curse."(2:15ff; 3:10) See an account of Pauline respect for the law and even for "rules" in Wayne Meeks, *The Origins of Christian Morality*, this chapter, note 7. James Carroll is also more nuanced on this subject; Paul, as a Pharisee "would have known that characterizations of Pharisaic piety as merely outward, as unconcerned with faith, as intrinsically hypocritical, were false" (Carroll, *Constantine's Sword*, p. 140).

What counts for my study is not the resolution of the Antioch confrontation and surely not of Paul's antinomianism; instead I want to show my reader how insistently the early Jesus movement—and with what narrative force!—denigrated the *keepers* of the law and the sacred biblical texts, texts that they, as "changed Jews," insisted on flexibly deforming.

20. Galatians 3:6–10 and 24. Levine and Brettler, *The Jewish Annotated New Testament*, point out that Paul here adds words ("the book") in verse 10 that are not in the original Hebrew from the Deuteronomic text (p. 337, n.10). It is one of many examples given in this edition of misquotations from the Hebrew Bible. See this chapter, note 8.

21. Ibid.

22. Meeks, *The Origins of Christian Morality*, p. 16; 208.

23. Meeks, lecturing at a symposium sponsored by the Yale Program on the Study of Anti-semitism, Whitney Humanities Center of Yale University, April 4, 2013.

24. Kermode, *The Genesis of Secrecy*, this chapter, note 7.

25. Barry S. Kogan, "Understanding Prophecy: Four Traditions," in Steven Nadler and T. M. Rudavsky, eds., *The Cambridge History of Jewish Philosophy* (New York: Cambridge University Press, 2009), pp. 481–82.

26. As Trude Weiss-Rosmarin, a Jewish educator, writer, and feminist, stated it plainly in 1943: "The chief and fundamental difference between Judaism and Christianity is that the former is committed to pure and uncompromising monotheism and the latter subscribes to the belief in the Trinitarian nature of the Divine Being. Trinitarianism, that is to say, the belief in and worship of 'God, the Son, and the Holy Spirit' are as basic and important to all types and denominations of Christianity as they are contrary to all and everything Judaism holds sacred. To the unconditional monotheism of Judaism the doctrine of the Trinity is profoundly objectionable, because … it is a concession to polytheism or, at any rate, an adulteration of the idea of the One, Unique, Indefinable, and *Indivisible* God." *Judaism and Christianity: The Differences* (New York: Jewish Book Club, 1943).

A. N. Wilson, speaking of the nonnegotiable aspects of Paul's Jewish contemporaries, allows that "there was no single monolithic entity at this period which one could label 'Judaism'; but there were millions of Jews [and] all subscribed to the notion that the God of Israel and the First Cause were one and the same being and that His laws had been dispensed to Moses on Mount Sinai and were inscribed in the Scriptures," *Paul: The Mind of the Apostle*, p. 6, note 18.

27. Hoenig, *The Essence of Talmudic Law and Thought*, p. 13, n. 12. It is true that Paul may be defended, interpretively, by seeing his technique as perhaps an extreme example of the "flexible" outer limit of such Talmudic techniques as *asmachta*—citing a Biblical text to support an external idea.

28. Bloom, *Jesus and Yahweh*, p. 44.

29. Kermode, *The Genesis of Secrecy*: "What Precisely Are the Facts?"

30. Littell, *The Crucifixion of the Jews*, passim.

31. Ibid, p. 26.

32. St. Augustine, *De Doctrina Christiana*, transl. *On Christian Doctrine* (New York: Dover, 2009), vol. 3, 5: 9. In these very sections, St. Augustine establishes certain rule of construction, certain boundaries for the interpretation of Scripture; but there is some irony in setting these down centuries after the "spirit-letter" textual divide had been forged.

33. Peter J. Tomson, *Paul and the Jewish Law* (Philadelphia: Fortress Press, 1990), "The Antioch Incident," pp. 222–30 at 224.

34. In the pages of the *New York Times*, the Chief Rabbi of the British Commonwealth, Jonathan Sacks, recently described the mix of endless debate with bounded, uncompromising vision within the Orthodox Jewish interpretive tradition: "The Torah is an anthology of argument with a shared vocabulary of common restraint," quoted by David Brooks, *New York Times*, March 8, 2013, p. A25.

35. "An eye for an eye"—viciously used across the centuries as a synonym for Jewish legal harshness—proved so mitigated by the universally understood tradition of its application (not to mention scriptural protections of criminal suspects) that a Jewish court that sentenced one person to death in seven (or some said seventy) years was nicknamed "the bloody Sanhedrin." See Jacob Neusner, *The Mishna: A New Translation* (New Haven, CT: Yale University Press, 1988), tractate Makkot 1:10, circa late second century CE. In other words, law and spirit, justice and mercy are *merged* within the long history of Jewish commentary, and the strict law that was viciously attacked over the course of the early Christian era was always already tempered with mercy. Part of this is the integration of the *oral tradition*, which is derived from the Torah in such sources as the Mishnah.

On the other hand, developments in Christian antinomianism based on the "spirit's" supposed fulfillment of the strict law have paradoxically led to far more literalism (and often cruelty) in the application of law during the Christian era. In this note I can only suggest as another book's subject the complex question of various Christian approaches to secular law. I point the reader, first, to Shakespeare's representation of Christian law in *The Merchant of Venice*; see this book, ch. 5, note 9, and see, e.g., Adam Seligman, "Love, Necessity, and Law in *The Merchant of Venice*," *J. of Scriptural Reasoning*, v. 11 (2012). See also here, ch. 5, note 9. For excellent recent tracking of the subjective and occasionally literalistic approaches to law among various Christian thinkers, see Karl-Heinz Ladeur and Ino Augsberg, " 'The Letter Kills, but the Spirit Gives Life?' On the Relevance of Jewish Concepts of Law for Postmodern Legal Theory," *Journal of Law and Religion* 36 (2010–11): "The law is never entirely available; it is only accessible and usable as it is actively interpreted and taught—since everything was 'already there' and will be there.... [whereas] in contrast [to] this Jewish conception, [for] the Christian construction, subjectivity has to be regarded as an 'autonomous source of spontaneity' as well as a 'self-producing activity.' It is conceived of as 'self determination,' eventually culminating in 'self-legislation.' This refers to a post-Pauline construction of law as an order that does not point to something other, something different from itself, but that refers to self-determination by the effort of one's own will" (pp. 436ff). Christian "law," divorced from a respect for the older legal tradition, becomes solipsistic; in its unbounded subjectivity, it depends in its application on the will of the adjudicator, which can move from one interpretive method to another depending on the outcome it wishes to reach. See this book, ch. 6, section (a).

36. Carroll, *Constantine's Sword*, e.g., pp. 39, 83–89, 138–40, 563ff. Carroll, who was trained as a Paulist, came to regret the effect over the centuries of Christian power in Europe, of the early texts about the Jews. He speaks of "the start-to-finish pattern in the Gospels of deflecting blame away from Romans and onto the Jews," tracking "through the lens of John" the "crystal clear" message that "the enemy of Jesus [was] the Jews."

4

Wartime France and the Occupied British Islands

Two Flexiphobes Unyieldingly Fight the Genocidal Trend and Are Joined by a Sitting Judge in Nazi Germany Itself

a. What Really Happened When France and the British Channel Islands Were Occupied

Everyone knows the story of France during World War II, or at least a caricature of it. The Germans overwhelm the French army, roll into France, and singlehandedly inflict four years of horrors on a defeated nation, which courageously tries to resist against overwhelming odds. The truer story, available and understood by now, even among Francophiles, places the resistance percentage at less than 5 percent and reveals that the worst part of the story—genocide—originated largely without any sustained German demand or active racial policy and emanated from a shady place called "Vichy," from which a largely autonomous French government promulgated 200 or so laws against the Jewish population on French soil; the Germans were delighted with the French approach to "the Jewish question" and imported it into the "occupied zone" as being wider and tougher in scope than many of their own racial laws.[1] This chapter emphasizes within the bigger story the intrangisent insistence of one man, Jacques Maury, who right at the start of his country's disastrous policies, wrote prominently that racial laws passed by a French government and implemented by French courts, administrators, and private lawyers ran totally counter to all French traditions and would therefore be ignored by any but the most flexible of French players. If the Nazis insisted on a racist policy—and if (as was unlikely) they could enforce it against an intractable population—well then perhaps the French could do little. But surely, as Maury felt soon after the fall of France and the publication of Vichy's first major racial statutes, the vast number of French people required to make such laws work would decline to do so. These policies and laws were grotesquely off the mark, he surmised, and they would immediately strike everyone in the French legal community as a bizarre and nonenforceable deviation from basic French law, even or especially in times of crisis and challenge.

Meanwhile, just west of French territory in the British Channel Islands, a far less well known part of wartime history was developing. Occupied by the Germans for a longer period than any other territory in Hitler's Europe, these islands found themselves urged to write and enforce anti-Jewish laws very similar to those in Vichy. What would the Britishers do, given their own traditions of due process, fairness, and stolidity when facing crises? Unhappily, British bureaucrats and lawyers caved malleably to the perceived emergency and began investigating and persecuting the Jewish islanders in their midst.[2] In the still very active governing body on the tiny island of Guernsey, on which a dozen suspected Jews were investigated by the island's authorities and three eventually deported to Auschwitz, only one Britisher—Sir Abraham Lainé—steadfastly spoke out against the publication and implementation of "Laws against the Jews"—an English language series of increasingly severe rules that shows us genocide reaching very far westward and into the discourse of our own mother tongue.

Herewith of the flexiphobes, Maury and Lainé, with a well-deserved coda about a sitting German judge, Lothar Kreyssig, who from a Nazi courthouse and into the early 1940s mounted "stiff-necked" protests against an entrenched tyrant about the lawlessness of euthanasia. None of these three was punished; all survived the war.

Herewith, too, of a most surprising offer made by the Vichy head of state—World War I hero Marshal Philippe Pétain—to the Vatican in 1941 to give him the church's direct advice on the religious acceptability of France's anti-semitic legislation. There was still time for a dramatic shift in France's policies, and Vichy's Catholic leader reached out for spiritual guidance from the "rock" of Vatican doctrine. He was to receive (and you will soon read) the church's response. He received it before any deportation trains had left France, carrying their eventual cargo of 75,000 Jews arrested under color of his regime's laws. During this key interval, the young professor, Jacques Maury, was using secular arguments to dissuade the Marshal from his course.

Professor Maury's inflexible insistence on fine French traditions of equality, and the sadly flexible Vatican response on the question of statist anti-semitism, tend forcefully to demonstrate that an individual organic fear of caving in leads to stalwart action that will be checked not so much by brutal governments as by mass indifference and a culture of compromise.

b. Professor Jacques Maury Courageously Publishes An Intransigent Protest against Vichy's Anti-Talmudism

1. A Scenario of Resistance in Newly Occupied Paris

Imagine yourself as a Parisian lawyer in late 1940, after the fall of France. You try to adjust to the Nazi jackboot. Like many of your compatriots, you do feel some normalcy returning to your life after the panic when the Germans rolled toward the capital.

You are back in your office, like most of your colleagues, and the practice is largely the same, before the same French courts, as it had been prior to the disaster.[3] You note the absence from the courts of a number of Jewish judges and lawyers, and you also see the peculiar new category of cases indexed as relating to "Juifs" ("Jews").

On the streets, the German occupier so far practices great courtesy to the defeated people. Life, apart from rationing and uncertainty, is actually good. The nightclubs are full again; Sartre and de Beauvoir are productive, in the theaters and on the radio.[4] Above all, perhaps, the beautiful capital city has been spared any widespread damage.

Catholic priests each Sunday are speaking to their flock—"Pétain's little parishioners," as they are being called—but their sermons would be mostly indistinguishable from prewar spiritual messages. There is scant reference to the increasingly obvious fact that some unfortunates are being rounded up in the streets and taken elsewhere, perhaps to one of many French-run "camps," perhaps abroad.

Occasional prelates broach the "Jewish question" through a "coded" language using "hidden" and "ambiguous" words and phrases. Lawyers in their pews might at best hear flexibly intended allusions, and rarely if ever direct calls in the name of charity to help the Jewish population on French soil:

> The message was that obedience to the gospels would set Europe free. Language as code, as prayers and sermons, and as images and gestures, was a potent force that, it could be argued, itself constituted spiritual resistance to nazification, if not a form of spiritual resistance.[5]

If you are an ordinary French lawyer sitting in your pew of a wartime Sunday, you might feel the balm of a "spiritual resistance" that was oblique and hardly called on you to speak clearly, much less to do anything.

If you are the specific lawyer named Professor Jacques Maury, you may be especially concerned that hard-wired French standards have been so quickly and easily traduced by Vichy leaders, who legislated against the Jews long before any Nazi pressure on them to do so.[6] You have flexiphobic inclinations, so you decide to speak out against these bizarre new laws. You pen for France's most prominent legal gazette, read by French leaders in both occupied Paris and Nazi-free Vichy, the following inspiring words of protest:

> The French people find themselves placed in three categories [Jewish citizens; foreign Jews on French soil/everyone else] of non-identical status. There is an increasing abandonment of our long-held rule safeguarding equality in their rights as well as their responsibilities to all French people.
>
> The legislator of 1940 goes much further [than any restrictive legislation passed before]. . . . He [i.e., the Pétain cabinet] opposes on principle one Frenchman from another; on the specific characteristic thus emphasized, the great majority of nationals are safeguarded rights that all the others, unless excepted, definitively and even retroactively lose. The notion of a quality indigenous to the person, of an essential quality has been substituted for or perhaps juxtaposed with that of a required progressive change. (*Journal officiel*, October 18, 1940)[7]

2. The Nonresponsiveness to Professor Maury

The young professor simply states what not only he but all French lawyers believe but no one else is saying publicly: however one may feel about Jews or other minorities, French law—"on principle"—

does not discriminate on the basis of racial, religious, or ethnic characteristics. He is confident his colleagues will adhere to those traditions, in place since 1789.

No one takes Maury out and shoots him. When it comes to indigenously powerful guilds such as law (or, say, religion), that is not the way things work, even in the most totalitarian of contexts. Maury continues to write about his regime's strange laws throughout the war, usually in a less flexiphobic way, trying to help beleaguered individuals avoid the hazardous status of Jew. His earlier direct reminder to his colleagues of basic French tradition has yielded to a more flexible rhetoric of working within the system. Maury has learned what the precious handful like him in Hitler's Europe also discovered: the challenge to these few intractable guardians of liberal European values arose not so much from tyrants as from their own colleagues.

Professor Maury was neither punished nor (sadly) endorsed by any government or collegial group. His insistence on the preservation of the traditional French "code" was not heeded by the legal community. His peers enjoyed, even amid the worst tyrants of the century, the same chance he had to protest directly against the bizarre, offensive new laws. Wartime history proves that even the Nazis could not shoot, or even punish substantially, a dissenting member of a powerful profession such as the law. This chapter's coda locates this proof within the Third Reich itself. Yet Maury's colleagues (almost to a man and woman) chose instead to cave flexibly, rejecting their training and traditions. Compromise of this sort, encouraged by specters of "emergency," often prevails. So it did in Vichy France.

Other law professors, lawyers, and judges, as well as most ordinary French people, had found a way into the "new Europe," whether by overt collaboration, silence, incremental participation in what became genocide, or some combination of all in the name of just learning to survive what they self-interestedly saw as someone else's problem. Was their underlying motivation outright racism, a visceral hatred of Jews? Xenophobia—there were so many foreign Jews on French soil, many of whom had fled from the east to the safe harbor of French traditions? Or, perhaps better, a deep resentment of Jews as Talmudists, as subject to other laws that compelled them to a greater faithfulness than the French were showing to their own traditions?

Whatever their motivation, at least some mainstream French men and women realized that adjustment in this case meant "rotten" compromise. A form of flexible deformation of ensconced textual understandings gradually permitted French lawyers, influenced by their religious leaders in many cases (the most infamous of which I shall shortly recount) to overcome their native aversion to indigenous anti-egalitarian laws against the Jews. To reach an eventual product of nearly 200 laws against Jews promulgated for the most part without significant German pressure and often surpassing through French "logic" even the Nazi racial precedents, French lawyers during World War II first needed to leap a hurdle not present in most other countries victimized by Hitler. They had to reckon with their ingrained belief in *egalitarianism*, a staple of the French legal system since 1789 and one that endured throughout the first decades of the twentieth century, turbulent years that included the Dreyfus trial (which did not, of course, involve any statist racial legislation).[8] The compromise with received codified meaning occurred over a four-year period, during which—with the help of that strange combination emphasized throughout this book of enlightenment compromise and Catholic hermeneutic flexibility—the French little by little degraded their traditional understandings of the word "equality." Under color of Vichy law, some 75,000 Jews were sent "to the East" and 3,000 more perished in French-run camps.

To produce within an entire community of lawyers a willingness to deform tradition and to compromise with such a key, ingrained feature of foundational French law, there had to be in place a *hermeneutic principle* of flexibility.[9] Somewhat akin to Gutmann and Thompson's norm for our world today discussed in Chapter 2, or that of St. Paul and St. John for the world of early Christianity discussed in Chapter 3, compromise, change, and quick departures from settled traditions became the rule.

Along the lines of the highly perceptive American TV commentator Bill Maher, "new rules" were being promulgated to fit the occasion,[10] and no one wanted to appreciate Professor Maury's public insistence upon a "return" to what had been sound and notable in French law.

c. The Vichy Leader Appeals to the Vatican

One man, the one who would be last on your list of likely Catholic resistance fighters, *was* worried about Vichy's increasing legislative program against Jews on French soil. Marshal Philippe Pétain, Vichy's octogenarian leader, had jumped the gun on any Nazi pressure whatsoever by promulgating anti-semitic laws as one of his government's first orders of business, in September and October 1940. A legalistic torrent followed, consisting of statutory and judicial activity relating to the Jews.

Amazingly, nine months or so into his own racist project, Pétain may have had misgivings. Perhaps his aging body called attention to the eventual fate of his immortal soul, but whatever the reason, this not particularly religious French Catholic commissioned an inquiry by his emissary to the Vatican to learn whether the church had any objections to Vichy's racist policies.

Leon Bérard, a talented lawyer and diplomat, spent the summer probing the church's attitudes. He heard from high Vatican officials that racism itself is unacceptable to the church. And that all those who had come to Christ, from whatever former level of substandardness, were equal in the eyes of the Faith. Maybe the church would advise Marshal Pétain that his laws were wrong in its eyes. The door was open for a response consistent both with morality and the church's own doctrine!

By September, Bérard had completed his survey of church officials. He wrote to Pétain. Consider the old French leader pondering the news from Rome. Without any Nazi intervention, his government in Vichy had already promulgated dozens of laws against the Jews. But so far, no deportation trains had rolled eastward from French soil. There was time for a turnaround in French law that would protect the Jews. There was time to change a flexible trend and to bring it back under the guidelines of French egalitarian traditions not even the Germans would have the manpower and treasure to overcome.

The old World War I hero had sought the Vatican's advice; what if the highest levels in Rome privately would tell him that his policies violated Catholic doctrine and placed his immortal soul at risk? *Didn't happen.* Marshal Pétain and his government would instead go on to draft another 150 laws and ordinances against the increasingly beleaguered Jews on French soil. Eventually, under color of French law, if you fit the legal definition of "Jew," you were isolated, robbed, terrorized, and then much worse.

I have studied Leon Bérard's lengthy letter to his leader. But each time I reread it, I stand amazed. Go ahead, he says to Vichy's leaders. Go ahead and isolate your Jews. Deprive them of their careers and their possessions. Put them in hideous prison camps within your country, knowing that many will die there. Accommodate even a worse fate for these people. It's OK. Regarding the ultimate victimization of the Jews, the church at its highest levels gives you not only the green light but also the comfort of its theological rest-stops along the way. The Vatican has taken a close look, and its clinical perspective lights your path toward genocide.

The Vatican's advice set up the ultimate flexible program, one reflective of the textual compromise and malleability that, as I have shown, dated back 2,000 years to the church's founders and sacred writers. Here are relevant passages from Bérard's letter to Pétain; it merits extensive citation, and key passages are highlighted:

2 September 1941. M. le Maréchal: By your letter of 7 August 1941, you honored me by requesting information touching questions and problems that might be raised, from the Roman Catholic perspective, by the measures your government has taken regarding the Jews. I have had the honor of sending you a preliminary response where I observed that nothing has ever been said to me at the Vatican that would imply, on the part of the Holy See, a critique or disapproval of those legislative and regulatory acts. Now I can affirm that at no time has the pontifical authority been either concerned or preoccupied with that part of French policies, and that no complaint or request coming to it from France has so far given it such an opportunity....

A. The Church and Racism. *There is a fundamental and basic opposition between Church doctrine and racist theories.* The Church, by universal definition, professes the unity of all human beings. The same Redeemer died for all men; the Gospel is announced to every creature....All these precepts are incompatible with a concept that could derive from the conformity of the skull and the nature of the blood and the aptitudes and the vocation of peoples, their religion itself, to establish finally a hierarchy of the races, at the top of which is found a pure and royal race called Aryan. [There are then quotations to this effect taken from the words of Pius XI in *Mit brennender Sorge* in 1937, as well as from other authoritative declarations.] The Church thus has condemned racism as it has condemned communism.

From its teachings about racist ideas one should be far from deducing, however, that it necessarily condemns any specific measure taken by any particular state against what it calls the Jewish race. Its thinking on this involves distinctions and nuances that must now be noted. The subject must be treated clearly.

B. The Church, the Jewish Problem, and Antisemitism.

It would be vain to extract from Canon Law, theology, pontifical acts, a group of precepts that resembles legislation on Judaism or the Judaic religion. It would even be difficult to find easily, regarding this subject, a clearly marked doctrinal body.

The first principle that appears, and the surest, is that in the eyes of the Church, a Jew who has been authentically baptized ceases to be a Jew and becomes part of Christ's flock. But one should not conclude from this that the Church regards religion alone as the thing marking Israel off in the midst of the nations. It does not believe that Jews constitute simply a spiritual family, as do in our case, for example, Catholics and reformed Christians. It recognizes that among the distinctive traits of the Jewish community there appear not so much *racial* as *ethnic* particularities. It discerned this long ago and has always taken this into account. [Bérard then recounts various periods in which such measures as the *numerus clausus* or special signs on apparel were adopted by Catholic authorities such as, respectively, St. Thomas of Aquinas and the Lateran Council.] ...

It would be possible now, with the help of these precedents, to determine whether the French laws on Jews contradict or not, and in what ways they contradict, Catholic tenets....

D. What Disjunctions Can One Find Between Catholic Doctrine and the French Law of 2 June 1941 on the Jews?

[Bérard reviews the law's exclusionary sections.] In principle, there is nothing in these measures that the Holy See would criticize. It believes that in promulgating such measures a State uses its legitimate power and that a spiritual force should not interfere with the internal politics of States. And, then too, the Church has never professed that the same rights must be given to or recognized in all citizens. It has never ceased teaching dignity and respect for the individual. But it surely does not understand matters in the fashion, strictly speaking, of the spiritual followers of Rousseau and Condorcet....Yet the law of 2 June 1941 begins with the legislator's giving a juridical definition of the Jew as expressly linked to the notion of race. Still, if we compare the law of 2 June with that of 3 October (which it replaced), we see that the new text has reduced the reliance on race. If a Jew proves that he belonged, prior to 25 June 1940, to the Catholic faith, or to the Calvinist or Lutheran faiths, he is no longer considered as a Jew, as long as he does not have more than two grandparents of the Jewish race. In this case, the law attached legal significance to conversion. *It remains the case that a Jew, if duly converted and baptized, will still be considered a Jew, if he is the issue of at least three grandparents of the Jewish race, that is having belonged to the Judaic religion.*

There, one must admit, is a contradiction between French law and Church doctrine.

E. Practical Result of This Contradiction. Conclusion. I just pointed out the sole point at which the law of 2 June 1941 contradicts a principle held by the Roman Church. *But it does not follow from this doctrinal divergence that the French state is threatened with...even a censure or disapproval that the Holy See might express in one form or another about the Jewish laws....As an authorized person at the Vatican told me, they mean no quarrel with the Jewish laws.* But a double wish has been expressed to me by the representatives of the Holy See, with the clear desire that it be submitted to the Head of State:

1) that no provision touching on marriage be added to the law on the Jews. There we would have difficulties of a religious nature. They were strongly moved at the Vatican when Romania adopted, on this vital point, legislation modeled on the Fascist laws;

2) that the precepts of justice and of charity be kept in mind in applying the law. My interlocutors seem to have had in mind particularly the liquidation of enterprises in which Jews have an interest....

Aside from these two caveats, it will be full speed ahead against the Jews. How does the church manage to announce and then violate its moral norm against racism in one and the same declaration? Bérard provides the answer toward the end of this section of his letter. The theological hairsplitting is essential both to the thesis of my book and (far more importantly) to the fate of Europe's Jews during World War II.

It is the epitome of flexibility, the carrying forward of two millennia of flexible thinking and morality. Bérard has been taught how opposites can simultaneously exist in church doctrine. He has been told, during that summer of 1941 when so much hinged on the teaching and when there was still time to reverse the awful flow of events, of *"an essential distinction that the Church has never ceased to admit and to practice, for it is full of wisdom and reason: the distinction between* thesis *and* hypothesis, *the thesis in which the principle is invariably affirmed and maintained and the hypothesis, where practical arrangements are organized."* In the space of this theological distinction, the church's alleged morality against racism can be made to accommodate to any given state's actual, racist legal practice. If events on the ground require the moral rule to be bent and perhaps broken, so be it. There is another rule—the "hypothesis"—that sculpts religious virtue into the base metal of *realpolitik*.

Bérard's letter apparently gave considerable solace to Pétain.[11] Although flagging the contradiction on the question of race, the letter not only denied its significance to the Vatican but, more important to our thesis, becomes a key working example of twentieth-century flexibility.

The obvious anti-Talmudism and statist racism were muted in this exchange of opinions on the Jewish laws. Emerging instead was a vitally significant mutual ability to engage in a flexible statecraft that masked persecution under the felt needs of the political moment. The hermeneutic of easy manipulation is ingrained in both entities.

We have seen that the great egalitarian foundations of France did not disappear overnight at the fall of France or when the Vichy régime took power. The ingrained political beliefs of tens of thousands of French people, beginning with Vichy's own leader, understood the departure from tradition represented by Vichy anti-Jewish legislation. The overt indication of this was Professor Maury's resistance to Nazi influence. Anti-semitism of various traditional kinds, and virulent racism, would not appeal to mainstream France.

Some far more native flexibility within their education would have to move them to make the system as pervasively anti-Jewish as it eventually became. Change of this magnitude would occur by appealing to a tradition that was far older than wartime France or even the kings of Gaul. It was the flexibility of those early Christian writers and texts, updated and retransmitted at the highest levels of European sectarian authority.

d. The British Channel Islands Fold, but One Flexiphobe Speaks Out

The wartime experience of the British Channel Islands governments replicated on a smaller scale that of the Vichy French authorities by whom they were strongly influenced. From July 1, 1940, until May 9, 1945, these islands, twelve miles or so west of France, endured the longest Nazi occupation of any other politically united territory in Europe.[12] There were the obvious similarities with all other wartime occupations—hardships on food and petrol rationing, communications restrictions, curfews. The similarity of greatest importance here is the adoption of an indigenous policy regarding the Jews, the question of how stable traditions of fair play bent and broke in the face of "the Jewish question," and the precious example of flexiphobic unwillingness to yield them even in an emergency. There were also unique features, of course: these Islanders, unlike the French, were part of a nation (Great Britain) that had not been vanquished by Hitler. Boosted perhaps by that thought, their morale was raised further by a kind of racial respect conveyed by the Nazis that was never given to the French or the Poles or the Russians. One wartime official on Guernsey, the channel island most central to our story, recalled that

> the German authorities had been instructed to treat the Guernsey people as being equal to the Germans from the point of view of culture and that they should, therefore, be treated with respect.... Hitler had also already set out his plans for a new Europe, based on racial theories which would render the whole of Eastern Europe liable to become a "service population" for the benefit of the "superior races." Included in these latter were the British.[13]

Their centuries-long ties with Great Britain and its traditions remained alive in the islanders' spirits, too, even though Churchill had bigger fish to fry and had abandoned trying to liberate them after a few very early abortive attempts.[14] They continued to rely—and the Germans permitted this—on indigenous governing bodies, especially each island's quasi-legislative, quasi-judicial Royal Court. Every issue of significance to islanders was vetted by these bodies and their Jurats, which issued policy opinions throughout the war that were then implemented by such long-standing island authorities as the Bailiff and the Attorney General. These authorities remained in place and, even though they had to reckon with the occupier's demands, they had a strong influence on the flow of events during those long years.

The islanders' response to the Nazis has been analyzed ever since the war, and there are sharply conflicting accounts.[15] Did they capitalize for their own comforts on the greater respect showed them as a racial matter? Was there widespread collaboration? Or was there significant resistance, in the spirit of their British traditions? As was true elsewhere under Hitler's yoke, did the islanders speak up forcefully on some issues while largely remaining silent (or worse, as we shall see) on others?

A litmus test to calibrate the backbone of the islanders, unsurprisingly, relates to the "Jewish question." There was a small number of Jews on the various islands—a total of sixteen on Jersey and Guernsey; a greater number of "suspected Jews" (a category that lawyers and bureaucrats thrived on, both in Vichy and the Channel Islands), and an even greater number of half-Jews sent from various places to do forced labor on the islands (especially Aldernay). Many half-Jews received "barbarous treatment."[16] Historians have been able to uncover the process leading to the legal categorization of indigenous Jews and eventually the deportation of some of them to Auschwitz.

Everyone agrees that the Royal Courts and Jurats played an active role in developing and promulgating anti-Jewish policies. In 1997, the *Oxford Companion to the Second World War* concluded that "some of the Islands' administrators collaborated with the Germans and helped in the round-up and deportation of Jews to concentration camps."[17]

It began as it always does in all genocides by defining (often through laws that look like any other) the group about to be isolated, robbed, imprisoned, and then if possible annihilated. I may have been one of the first researchers to find primary documentation related to the islands that is connected to the process of ferreting out Guernsey's Jewish population for such treatment. While concluding my archival work on Vichy France, I was surprised to discover English-language files touching on wartime "racial definition." They were from Guernsey and suggested a flexible integration on that Island of British legal and administrative traditions into the search for and punishment of those suspected of being Jews.[18]

On April 24, 1941, an article was published in the standard newspaper on Guernsey. Along with cigarette ads and other notices, it set forth an official version of the Island's approach to its Jews:

> Any person having at least three grandparents of pure Jewish blood shall be deemed to be a Jew. A Jewish grandparent having belonged to the Jewish religion shall be deemed to be of pure Jewish blood.
>
> Any person having two Jewish grandparents of pure Jewish blood who (a) at the time of the publication of this Order, belongs to the Jewish religious community or who subsequently joins it, or (b) at the time of the publication of this Order is married to a Jew shall be deemed a Jew.
>
> In doubtful cases, any person who belongs or has belonged to this Jewish religious community shall be deemed a Jew.[19]

The publication let everyone know that the Jew, as so defined along the lines of Vichy models, was barred from all kinds of economic activities. Worse still was in store; eventually three of Guernsey's Jews were deported to Auschwitz, under color of the island's laws.

But before that happened, the islanders through their official deliberative body had a chance to speak up. The content of the Jewish laws invited official islander commentary and seemed to need the Jurat's consent; the issue was going to be debated. Historian David Fraser concluded in his landmark study:

> The documentary record on which this book is based now clearly and beyond question establishes that high-ranking government, police, and bureaucratic officials in Jersey and Guernsey participated wholeheartedly and almost without question in the persecution of resident Jews and in the programme of Aryanization aimed at the exclusion of Jewish economic and business interests.[20]

When Fraser says "almost without question," he is pointing to the exceptional case, the stiff-necked reminder to all others of British tradition, a person recognized by other historians of Guernsey as well. A member of the long-standing administrative bodies and a non-Jew, his name was Abraham Lainé.

At a meeting of the Guernsey deliberative body, Bailiff Ambrose J. Sherwill and Inspector W. R. Sculpher—among the highest ranking island officials during the war—constituted the voices of majoritarian flexibility in the face of laws like these, so antithetical to British traditions:

> When Sherwill explained his reasons for not raising objections to the registration of the first anti-Jewish order put before the Royal Court, he felt "no purpose" would be served

in advising the Royal Court to refuse to register it.... But Sir Abraham Lainé openly and categorically refused his assent, and stated his grave objections to such a measure.... [Lainé's protest] turned no votes.[21]

Postwar, Sherwill confessed that during Lainé's persistent objections to placing the Jurat's imprimatur on strange laws isolating Guernsey's Jews, he realized that Lainé was right but said nothing to support his colleague:

As I sat listening to him, I realized how right he was.[22]

Flexibility always gets things "right" after the fact, and the fact, sometimes, is immeasurable and irreversible harm to those sacrificed to the malleable moment. We can again, wrongly in my view, impute the silence of Lainé's colleagues to actual anti-semitism in these people, but this is probably not a dominating reason, and Lainé's unpunished behavior indicates that it was probably not fear either. On Guernsey, as in France, a good explanation besides flexibility in the face of "emergency" might be the delight lawyers take in parsing, with infinite dexterity, legal texts such as the Guernsey statute that have "gray areas" in them such as what happens to people with mixed grandparental heritage? Questions like that keep lawyers and bureaucrats busy and supplement other benefits to the mainstream community of eliminating Jewish business competitors.[23]

More edifying would be to ask about the steadfast one: what wellspring of stolidity, what inner voice saying "This far you can push me, but no further," what intractability, motivated a man like Lainé to say "No" to his flexible colleagues? Indeed, he spoke publicly to the Germans as well, as he had done relating to the occupier's attempted slaughter of all cattle on the island or the assessment of a lower butter/egg ration. Lainé protested against all of these. On the butter/egg issue, Lainé, with his colleagues' full support, "argued with the Commandant for three hours"[24] and apparently gained a measure of success. Without his flexible colleagues, however, Lainé was helpless on the "Jewish question".

Lainé seemed to have internalized a kind of organic impulse that rebelled against the "spineless"[25] attitude of his compatriots toward the Germans; but, like Jacques Maury when he stood alone on the Jewish issue, Lainé was defeated. Flexiphobic responses against grotesque manipulation of fine traditions fail because natural allies fold their tents. It always takes more than one, unless you have the force and full control over destiny of a Sully Sullenberger; whole communities must "work out" together, must exercise their habituation over and over again to ensure what I am calling the intransigent response when it is most needed. But each person with the steadfastness of a Maury or a Lainé will endeavor to awaken the dormant spirit he knows lies just under the surface of his colleagues' complacent caving.

e. Intractable Devotion to Pre-Hitler Legal Traditions: A Wartime German Judge Speaks Up

Where there is solidarity among those rigidly upholding the good, as in the French Protestant town of Chambon sur Lignon, or in Denmark, or in pre-Nazi occupied Italy, even the most seemingly impenetrable of tyrants can be forced to stand down. Perhaps hoping to find such solidarity within the belly of the beast itself, a judge on the German Court of Guardianship in Brandenburg publicly protested against some of Hitler's cruelest policies. Postwar historian Ingo Mueller calls this the "one documented case of resistance in which a judge [Lothar Kreyssig] opposed the system in the course of following out his professional duties."[26] Like Professor Jacques Maury, whose protest against

French departures from fine legal traditions were penned at roughly the same time as Kreyssig's, the judge endeavored publicly to reawaken in his colleagues and superiors their advanced intuition about right and wrong in German legal traditions. His firm Lutheran beliefs apparently played a role.

Not surprisingly given the main themes of this chapter and book, Kreyssig did not depend on "natural law" or some flexible supra-legal theory to undermine what passed for Nazi law. To the contrary, he was a strict *positivist*, meaning a judge who was trained to follow the law-on-the-books, not get around it. Indeed, he abhorred precisely the extreme *flexibility* of Nazi courts. Crafted to do the will of the Fuehrer, Nazi law had been debased by the high-level theories of Hitler's jurisprudential guru, Carl Schmitt, who had long ago formally declared an end to the very idea of sticking to the text of the law.[27] From the beginning of the Hitler period on, judges were instructed to be "creative"; even when the law said the opposite, they were told to hand down verdicts that they felt and sensed would please Hitler.

Judge Kreyssig would not tolerate this debasing of German legal rules and traditions. He began issuing injunctions to several hospitals in his jurisdiction preventing them from pursuing the Nazi policies on euthanasia. He brought criminal charges against a Nazi party leader who had been responsible for that program. He wrote a long flexiphobic letter to the president of the Prussian Supreme Court objecting to the entire approach to law—which he in as many terms labeled "flexible"—of the Third Reich.

> "Whatever benefits the people is lawful." In the name of that terrible doctrine, which has yet to be contradicted by those whom it behooves to protect the law in Germany, entire areas of communal life have been placed beyond the reach of the law—the concentration camps for example, and now institutions for the mentally ill as well.[28]

Kreyssig was not taken out and hanged on meat hooks—we are seeing that lawyers, priests, and other powerful figures protesting within their professional capacity are just not treated that way and that even tyrants must respond cautiously to embedded power groups—Kreyssig accepted retirement at full pension in 1942. He was able to discuss his experiences with many audiences after the war. They are inspiring.

Unfortunately for the potential reversal of history that following his lead might have accomplished, no one jumped on his bandwagon.

What mechanism explains Europe's utter abandonment of its basic cultural values during the Holocaust? Fear? Perhaps; but close studies such as ours here about Vichy and Guernsey indicate—as did the precious example of Lothar Kreyssig—that direct protesters, standing alone, were not killed, punished, or even professionally sanctioned. Traditional anti-semitism? Perhaps; but much of enlightened Europe—although itself also subject to excess flexibility[29]—had long ago given up its most flagrant anti-Jewish attitudes. The best answer lies at the core of this book's thesis: an almost infinite ability to compromise values was deeply embedded in two millennia of European thought and practice. We saw this in the Vatican's response to Marshal Pétain and in the willingness of an entire caste of hitherto proudly positivistic judges in Germany to yield to their subjective desire to be true not to their training but to faith in the Fuehrer. When continental wartime flexibility looked at the Jew in their midst, even the least racist and xenophobic among them saw the intolerably lasting example on earth of a people true to their heritage, their law, their best traditions.

It was this form of anti-semitism—call it anti-Talmudism[30]—that perhaps most helps us to understand liberal Europe's reticence in the face of Hitler. The flexible simply do not take well to the seemingly inflexible ones, to the intransigent.

Notes

1. Michael Marrus and Robert Paxton, *Vichy France and the Jews,*
passim; Richard Weisberg, *Vichy Law and the Holocaust in France* (New
York: New York University Press, 1996), ch.2.

2. David Fraser, *The Jews of the Channel Islands and the Rule of Law*
(Brighton, UK: Sussex Academic Press, 2000), 1940–45.

3. See Weisberg, *Vichy Law,* chapter 8, for an account from the archives
of the relative normalcy of a lawyer's life in Occupied Paris.

4. Herbert Lottman, *The Left Bank: Writers, Artists, and Politics from the
Popular Front to the Cold War* (Chicago: University of Chicago Press, 1982).

5. See Vesna Drapac, *War and Religion, Catholics in the Churches of Occupied Paris* (Washington, DC: Catholic University of America Press,
1998), also cited at chapter 1, note 5. Drapac's sympathetic approach to
the church on the parish level cannot mask troubling themes central to
not only this chapter but my study as a whole:

> The language that is peculiar to the Church must be understood if its
> pronouncements are to be appreciated fully. It constitutes a sort of
> code, and one must have the key to the code. Much in that language
> was not new but developed new significance in changed circum-
> stances. Some was deliberately unspecific—often the occupation was
> referred to as "the current situation" or the ordeal—though Catho-
> lics listening or reading the messages knew what was meant....
>
> [M]eanings were "hidden" or "ambiguous" only to those unfamiliar
> with the language's devices. Under authoritarian regimes (in this
> case an occupation regime) language becomes complicated....The
> message was that obedience to the gospels would set Europe free.

6. All authorities are in accord on Vichy's autonomy in 1940 and 1941
on "the Jewish question." "Any simple notion of German *Diktat* can be
dismissed summarily," Marrus and Paxton, *Vichy France and the Jews,*
p. 5; Philippe Verheyde, *Les Mauvais Comptes de Vichy* (Paris: Perrin,
1999), p. 23; Weisberg, *Vichy Law,* chapter 2.

7. The *Journal officiel* was then and is today the official compendious
reporter of French laws, cases, and commentaries such as Maury's here
to the new Vichy laws of October 3–4, 1940, relating to the Jews. Unlike
any other country in Occupied Europe, this journal continued without
interruption to report during the entire war, and anyone picking the

volumes up from 1940 to 1944 would only see as different the index category "Juifs."

8. For a leading work on the Dreyfus affair, see Vincent Duclert, *Alfred Dreyfus, L'Honneur d'un Patriote* (Paris: Fayard, 2006); see also note 29.

9. Weisberg, *Vichy Law,* pp. 54–55.

10. Bill Maher has his own show on HBO, which has a segment called "new rules." He seems to have a special feel for religious hypocrisy, and even made a film about it. He stated recently: "Some people think the Catholic Church is based on the words of Jesus; in fact, like this show's writers, it's just a bunch of guys sitting around and creating 'new rules'" (March 28, 2013).

11. Marrus and Paxton, *Vichy France and the Jews,* p. 202, note 1.

12. For competent accounts of the wartime Channel Islands, see, e.g., Barry Turner, *Outpost of Occupation* (London: Aurum Press, 2010); Hazel R. Knowles Smith, *The Changing Face of the Channel Islands* (New York: Palgrave, 2007).

13. Smith, *The Changing Face,* 21–22.

14. Smith, *The Changing Face,* 13; Turner, *Outpost of Occupation,* p. 2.

15. Contrast the balanced but generally complimentary account of the islanders in Turner, *Outpost of Occupation,* with the scathing criticisms by Madeleine Bunting in *The Model Occupation* (UK: Harper Collins, 1995), which created something of a furor by characterizing the islanders' attitude as "one of compromise. They were more quiescent than other Europeans. They did as they were told." Smith, *The Changing Face,* p. xviiii. See also *The Oxford Companion to the Second World War,* which devotes exactly half of its meager account of the Channel islanders to their "collaboration."

16. See, e.g., Turner, *Outpost of Occupation,* p. 144.

17. Reported at Smith, *The Changing Face of the Channel Islands,* p. xviii.

18. See Weisberg, "In Defense of *Flexiphobia*: How Training in Intractability Can Help Lawyers in Moments of Perceived Emergency," 33 *Cardozo Law Review* 101 (2012). The case of an innkeeper on Guernsey, revealed in that file, became the subject of a kind of Milgram-like experiment I conducted with hundreds of lawyers through the years. Fully 80 percent of them, asked to role play as the legal decision maker in Mrs. Woolnaugh's case, decline to take the opportunity—set up for them by reminding them they had been trained in Anglo-American traditions of

due process and presumption of innocence—to challenge the anti-Jewish laws directly and unequivocally.

19. For the comprehensive volume on the Islands' anti-Jewish statutes and their systematic implementation by island officials and lawyers, see Fraser, *The Jews of the Channel Islands and the Rule of Law*, e.g. chapter 2, "The Jew as Legal Subject."

20. Ibid., p. 2.

21. Turner, *Outpose of Occupation*, p. 167.

22. Smith, *The Changing Face of the Channel Islands*, p. 144.

23. For an example of how even contemporary American lawyers have "fun" parsing wartime racial statutes on very low levels of flexibly creative analysis, see note 16. See also this book, ch. 1, note 3.

24. Alice Evans, ed., *Guernsey under Occupation: The Second World War Diaries of Violet Carey* (Stroud, Gloucestershire, UK: Phillimore, 2009).

25. Fraser, *The Jews of the Channel Islands*, p. 149 and his n.15.

26. See Ingo Mueller, *Hitler's Justice: The Courts of the Third Reich* (1991), pp. 193–95. Judge Kreyssig was unique, but American scholar Matthew Lippmann reports that as late as 1942, other members of the judiciary protested Hitler's incursions on the German tradition of an independent judiciary. See Lippmann, "Law, Lawyers, and Legality in the Third Reich," 13 *Temple International and Comparative Law Journal* 11 (1997): 238–40.

27. Schmitt's 1932 statement that "the era of legal positivism has come to an end" is quoted in Mueller, *Hitler's Justice*, at p. 219. Schmitt's jurisprudential approach, which sometimes associated Jewishness with a "positivistic" tendency to stick to the text, is reported, and then analyzed superbly, in Michael Stolleis, *The Law under the Swastika; Studies on Legal History in Nazi Germany* (trans. by Thomas Dunlop, 1998) (Chicago: University of Chicago Press, 1998).

28. Mueller, *Hitler's Justice*, at p. 194.

29. See, e.g., Chapter I, n. 7. The failures of enlightenment thought during periods of emergency (including the Vichy period and its predecessor in the Dreyfus Affair) are explicitly treated throughout this book but merit the interested reader's attention to much more elaborate analyses such as in Pierre Birnbaum's superb *Les Fous de la Republique* (Paris: Fayard, 1992) or Denis Bredin's *The Affair: The Case of Alfred Dreyfus* (trans. Jeffrey Mehlman [New York: Braziller, 1986]).

30. Weisberg, *Vichy Law*, chapters 2 and 10.

5

Secular Storytellers Present the Limits of Compromise

Shakespeare, Glaspell, and Faulkner

While philosophical and religious traditions urged large numbers of people toward flexibility, the first by appealing to reason and the second to faith-based skepticism of "pharisaic" intransigence, stories from Shakespeare to the present have largely seen the downside of infinite openness. We should not be surprised to find secular stories joining with the sacred and secular in elaborating the themes of this book. For only through stories, really, can so many of us be shocked from our patterns of thought and even our quotidian vocabulary into restorative habits of mind and practice.

A literary tradition begins with *Hamlet*, where the Prince of Denmark's otherwise compelling trait of quick-witted maneuverability runs afoul of an unchanging and righteous command. It follows here with an insufficiently recognized masterpiece, Susan Glaspell's "A Jury of Her Peers" (1919), where two women stand in solidarity against a male-dominated legal world that prefers sustaining its own dominance to searching for justice. Glaspell's notion that "outsiders" to law and authority may see things more clearly than princes and district attorneys is elaborated three decades later in the racially charged atmosphere of William Faulkner's deep south. *Intruder in the Dust* repetitively insists to any sentient reader that the hitherto negative trait of "intractability" deserves our admiration and even imitation; Faulkner's beleaguered man of color—falsely accused and threatened with lynching—stands (stead)fast, and with the help of three other "outsiders" treads the difficult but righteous path to factual truth and legal exoneration.

1. Thinking too precisely on th'event: Hamlet Flirts with Flexiphobia

Who has not thought about Shakespeare's troubled prince, and who has not needed to work through at least some of the many questions he ponders? "To be or not to be?"—the most famous of these—asks whether to sustain a life defined by a slumberous incapacity to act. "Conscience," he surmises, "doth make cowards of us all" because sometimes excess reflection dims our allegiance to "enterprises of great pith and moment." For Hamlet the crucial question has become whether he will summon the fortitude needed to rid both the Danish throne of a murderous mediocrity (Claudius) and his mother (Gertrude) of a lecherous bedmate wholly unworthy of her. Hamlet responds affirmatively early in the play when his noble father's ghost gives him the "horrible" news that the new king has killed him to gain, corruptly, both his crown and his wife. The ghost enjoins his son to avenge that murder and to set the public and private Denmark right.

The ghost's terms have merely confirmed what Hamlet's "prophetic soul" already knew. He will act not in a knee-jerk manner but according to the judgment already deeply ingrained within the core of his being. He will inspire others through his example of loyalty to a righteous command. He will "leap" to his revenge and in the process liberate Denmark from a "rotten" upstart. The ghost enjoins his loving son to "remember me." And so it will surely be, given Hamlet's utter faith in what his beleaguered late father has revealed to him alone; his innately sound response shows that Hamlet flirts with intransigence at the beginning of the play. His "advanced intuition" resonates harmoniously with the specter's marching orders:

> *O! My prophetic soul! . . .*
> *. . . Remember thee!*
> *Ay, thou poor ghost, whiles memory holds a seat*
> *In this distracted globe. Remember thee!*
> *Yea, from the table of my memory*
> *I'll wipe away all trivial fond records,*
> *All saws of books, all forms, all pressures past,*
> *That youth and observation copied there;*
> *And thy commandment all alone shall live*
> *Within the book and volume of my brain,*
> *Unmix'd with baser matter.*[1] *(I, v)*

Hamlet is up to the task. No wilting violet, he is by all accounts—from his girlfriend Ophelia's to the fierce avenger Fortinbras's at the play's very end—born and bred to royal action. He decides, though, to become a compromiser, to negotiate the ghost's text and to put it through the ringer of almost endless analysis. Seconds after uttering the noble speech just quoted, he begins the long process of unwinding and equivocating a pure thought.

We may like Hamlet just because he must make the situation his own. Ultimately, our judgment of his willful delay decides for each of us whether we ourselves, in whatever comparable challenges enter our lives, become a Neville Chamberlain of prevarication or a Winston Churchill of uncompromising resolve. What the text tells us beyond question is that Hamlet eventually realizes that he has overcomplicated, fatally, the pure thought that was his original response. It is not so much hesitation as the rendering complex that is the very hallmark of flexibility. His hesitation costs the lives of many innocent others: Polonius, Ophelia, Rosencrantz, Guildenstern, Gertrude, and Laertes all die before the attractively flexible prince dispatches the villainous Claudius and then dies himself.

In our terms, Hamlet epitomizes the turn of mind of many highly creative characters before and since: he has become habituated to malleable compromises of principle and not to what Elaine Scarry calls a beneficial "rigidity" in emergency situations such as the one he faced. Another way of thinking through his behavior would be to consider him a violator of a *just code*. The way a good law appeals to people's reason and to their emotions, what the ghost dictates to him makes total sense. Like a dog owner enjoined by a good law to clean up after his canine, or a motorist to put on the safety belt, or even reluctant consumers of cigarettes or humongous sweet sodas, Hamlet knows, through and through, that the ghost's code is harmonious with his deepest sense of right and wrong. He violates the code in the name of thinking things through for himself. Who can criticize him for being so "modern"—and he thinks out loud with such beauty, letting us in on his struggle! But we find out during the play that he always knew he should have been "going backward" to the ghosts' code.

Toward the end, Hamlet places the blame on himself and on his endless ability to equivocate; in his final soliloquy, Hamlet articulates brilliantly the thesis of this book:

> *How all occasions do inform against me,*
> *And spur my dull revenge! . . .*
> *Sure he that made us with such large discourse,*
> *Looking before and after, gave us not*
> *That capability and god-like reason*
> *To fust in us unused. Now whether it be*

> *Bestial oblivion, or some craven scruple:*
> *Of thinking too precisely on th'event,*
> *A thought which, quarter'd, hath but one part wisdom*
> *And ever three parts coward, I do not know*
> *Why yet I live to say "This thing's to do,"*
> *Sith I have cause and will and strength and means*
> *To do't. (IV,iv,30 ff.)*

Several images close to the heart of the present study grab our attention as Hamlet seizes the reason for his fatal hesitancy before his evil uncle's fratricidal corruption. "Thinking too precisely on th'event"—how richly this one phrase describes the maneuverability of St. Paul and St. John with Jewish texts that had long stood for one thing but now were being bent out of shape; or of Justice Scalia's intense effort—critiqued shortly in these pages—to make the Second Amendment say that which it does not; or of our own all-too-human proclivity to rationalize inaction! Flexibility has its enormously creative and attractive side; but Hamlet's endless arrangement of reality to delay his just revenge shows us the failure of excessive analysis when other, more flexiphobic approaches manage to get good work done through a deceptively simple path to rightness.

Hamlet in Act I knows in his heart of hearts and in his excellent brain that the ghost's command to kill Claudius is righteous, sound, and completely akin to his own deepest awareness. But the later Hamlet has figuratively "quartered" the pure thought his earlier and best self vowed to privilege over all "baser" distractions.

"A thought once quartered"—if it is a good thought by our own lights—"hath but one part wisdom/And ever three parts coward." So, perhaps, Chamberlain at Munich. Prince Hamlet concludes that some thoughts deserve our total commitment; should we not also cultivate and make habitual the thoughts and practices that are dear to us? Flexibility takes us from that habit to the endless openness that, in times of high moral and political challenge, can debase our lives.

This is Hamlet's awareness. It comes too late, for the stage has been strewn with (the wrong) bodies.[2]

2. Susan Glaspell's Women Bond to Do the Right Thing

"A Jury of Her Peers" is a small early twentieth-century American masterpiece.[3] Glaspell based her story on two actual legal decisions, neither explicitly cited of course in this imaginative tale that began as a short play called *Trifles*. A US Supreme Court decision lay on one end of the spectrum Glaspell could have conjured;[4] and on the other hand was a more local case she had covered as a journalist at the turn of the century: *State of Iowa v. Margaret Hossack*.[5] A still larger background had been sketched by the woman's suffrage movement. Glaspell's narrative recounts swiftly and brilliantly the emergence of two small-town women into the world of law otherwise dominated by myopic and wrongly motivated men. As classic "outsiders" to a law that had become overburdened with wrong-headed subjective biases, these women move in flexiphobic unity to defend the life of a neighbor who has apparently strangled her husband.

Minnie Foster's husband has been found dead, lying in the couple's bed with a rope around his neck, and there are no signs of forced entry or anyone else being in the house at the time of death. Minnie has been arrested and, while she has not confessed, neither has she said anything to exonerate herself. The sheriff has put her in jail, and now he and the county attorney return to her house to investigate. They are accompanied by the farm lady Mrs. Hale and the sheriff's wife, Mrs. Peters, both of whom the law officers relegate to the kitchen while they go off in search of clues as to Minnie's motive. All the action takes place in that quintessential feminine "sphere."

If Hamlet's equivocation in the face of injustice leads to the death of many innocent others, Mrs. Hale and Mrs. Peters discover a common moral grounding in order to save the life of Minnie Foster. They transform the only space allowed them into a laboratory of forensic investigation; and while the men search self-confidently but futilely for "hard-nosed" evidence, the women gradually bond to protect the accused. Only their alertness, coupled with their gradual willingness to stand together for steadfastness, translates the signs of Minnie's abuse into the tacit defense that will gain a name much later but that the Iowa judge had also anticipated: "battered woman syndrome."

This is a story that, in our terms, pits one flexiphobia against another. Recall that it is always much better for our deeply held position to have an opponent whose views are on the table than to deal with a shifty, covert foe who is hiding his motives. The male officers of the law in *Jury*—like the racist potential lynch mob in the Faulkner story I treat next—leave no doubt as to their perspectives on the case: Minnie is guilty, and they need only to find a motive, without which it is unlikely a jury will convict any woman. The men's self-assured absolutism helps the women better to figure out and to make palpable their own deepest feelings.

On the other hand, Mrs. Hale and Mrs. Peters begin the story neither as allies nor activists. Their roles, respectively, as farmer and sheriff's wife disincline them to radical departures from what was expected of women. Many had failed before them to leave any imprint on the law. Women had been ejected from the sphere of law not only by custom and statute but also by the Constitution itself. True enough, just after the Civil War, an "equal protection clause" had been added, which appeared on its own plain terms to protect women from legalized discrimination:

XIV. . . . nor shall any person be deprived of the equal protection of the law.

But the Fourteenth Amendment was being interpreted with great dexterousness by white male Supreme Court justices bent on using "the nature of things" to trump text and intended policy and to segregate blacks in public places and to confine women to their kitchens. So, forty years or so before the publication of Glaspell's story, Supreme Court Justice Bradley had found a way to keep a lawyer, Myra Bradwell, from the practice of law in Illinois; in doing so, he becomes the first but not the last Supreme Court justice in my study to have missed the boat badly when asked to find the meaning of a contested constitutional provision:

> Man is, or should be, woman's protector and defender. The natural and proper timidity and delicacy which belongs to the female sex evidently unfits it for many of the occupations of civil life. The constitution of the family organization, which is founded in the divine ordinance, as well as *in the nature of things*, indicates the domestic sphere as that which properly belongs to the domain and functions of womanhood. [The] paramount destiny and mission of woman are to fulfill the noble and benign offices of wife and mother. This is the law of the Creator. [emphasis added][6]

Excessive interpretive flexibility rears its head in this passage. Somewhat like the early Christian interpreters of the Jewish Bible, Justice Bradley turns the Fourteenth Amendment into a kind of allegory of its plain meaning. This can be dangerous, because one man's wild view of things gets imputed to a text that seems utterly to resist such a perspective. Of course, "equal protection of the law" required interpretation: was it meant, for example, to forbid ordinary statutes that treat one person worse than another, like a law requiring store front eye care to have an ophthalmologist on site, thus disadvantaging opticians wishing to deal directly with the public? Or a law requiring stores to be closed on Sundays? Or dog owners to be more scrupulously clean on city streets than other pedestrians? But did that need for interpretation liberate Justice Bradley to impute his own "women belong in the kitchen" mentality to the entire country?

Against such a background, women at the time of the story could not count on too much support from the genteel and paternalistic legal order. They needed *to work together*. We have seen in considering France, Guernsey, and Germany during World War II that solitary action in the service of the just will likely fail, and that a community is needed when protest against legalized ills emerges. Glaspell doubles down on that recognition, and the short story masterfully shows how two very different kinds of women, faced with a challenge, can reach way down to some common stopping place, to some "rigidity," that fights against wrongdoing.

Mrs. Hale is a sturdy and fairly independent farm woman, while Mrs. Peters is a frail, unassuming sheriff's wife—"married to the law," as she informs Mrs. Hale, whom she hardly knows prior to these events. As they peruse Minnie's kitchen, these unlikely allies begin quite far apart:

> "You know"—[Mrs. Hale] paused, and feeling gathered—"It seems kind of *sneaking*; locking her up in town and coming out here to get her own house to turn against her!" "But Mrs. Hale," said the sheriff's wife, "the law is the law."

They gradually begin, however, to "see" things together. Something lies in that "separate sphere" that will tell the absent and mute Minnie Foster's story; a piece of sewing stitched crazily out of place—maybe Minnie's last act of domesticity—signals a moment that only they will manage to reconstruct, without revealing it to the men. Upon further discovery of an empty bird cage, the women build on a memory of a young and joyful Minnie who herself used to sing like a bird before her cold marriage—in their imaginations—crushed her spirit:

> "Look at the door," [Mrs. Peters] said slowly. "It's broke. One hinge has been pulled apart." Mrs. Hale came nearer. "Looks as if someone must have been—rough with it." Again their eyes met—startled, questioning, apprehensive...

If Minnie did strangle her husband in his bed, the women know now it is because she has been abused. They have no vocabulary for this, however. Only much later in the twentieth century does "battered woman syndrome" appear as a possible defense. Mrs. Peters and Mrs. Hale recognize that the discovery by the lawmen of a cruel husband would supply the motive a jury will need *to convict* a wife, otherwise an unlikely candidate at the time for arrest and trial. Indeed, Glaspell's reportage of the Iowa case taught her that someone like Minnie—if brought to trial for the murder of her husband—will ultimately be exonerated if the defense mutes that abuse, leaving the prosecution without sufficient motive to convict. (In *Hossack*, the state's highest court reversed a conviction for lack of a motive when it found insufficient evidence of a long pattern of abuse.) Where today, thanks to such stories and legal developments, a jury might be responsive to a battered woman whose justification for violence falls short of self-defense, Mrs. Peters and Mrs. Hale know that once Minnie is taken from her kitchen into the male world of physical violence, she is lost in every sense.

What are the women to do? It takes less than two pages of narrative, given the longer work of bonding that has already taken place, for them to take the jury function onto themselves. (I won't give away the details, hoping my readers will engage this insufficiently read masterpiece on their own.) Whether today's reader agrees or disagrees with what the women wind up doing, their tacit incursion into the "sphere" of justice can only be thought of as a flexiphobic response, an organic seeing through to what they know is right.

Mrs. Hale and Mrs. Peters "over-rule" *Bradwell v. Illinois*. They "restore" justice.

3. "Intractability" and Faulkner's Heroic Lucas Beauchamp

William Faulkner expressed a persuasive preference
for the immensely varied stories of the Hebrew Bible
as compared with the Greek New Testament...
            (*Harold Bloom*, JESUS AND YAHWEH)

No recent story better evokes the power of an unyielding and calm steadfastness than Faulkner's *Intruder in the Dust*. In a tale that also quickly implicates the need for "outsider justice" in the amassing of evidence, a black prisoner awaits possible lynching. He has been found near the body of a white man, in the deep Jim Crow South, and he is holding a (literal) smoking gun. Yet this un-likely protagonist, Lucas Beauchamp, calmly manages from the jailhouse an investigation into his own guilt or innocence. Facing the rednecked rage of flexiphobic opponents, he stays on target throughout, assessing who are his natural allies and summon-ing them because he knows they share his urge to find out the truth.

Remarkable in such a relatively short novel, the word "intractable" appears seven times (often coupled with the word "composed")—

and the word "inflexible" thrice—in descriptions of Lucas Beauchamp. The unique power of such stories involves changing the meaning of the words we use, upgrading the pejorative and challenging us to critique our own flexible habits of mind. Here are a few examples of this Faulknerian "leitmotif," a repetitious verbal melody about a magnificent man of color that stays in our mind like a theme in a Beethoven symphony; each recurring, inflexible intonation is uttered narratively by the adolescent Chick Mallison: [7]

> ...a face which...might have been under fifty or even forty except for the hat and the eyes, and inside a Negro's skin but that was all...because what looked out of it had no pigment at all, not even the white man's lack of it, not arrogant, not even scornful: just intractable and composed. (p. 7)
>
> [four years later,]...Lucas was living alone in the house, solitary kinless and intractable, apparently not only without friends even in his own race but proud of it.... (p. 23)
>
> Then the rear door opened and the sheriff emerged—a big, a tremendous man with no fat and little pale eyes in a cold almost bland pleasant face who without even glancing at them turned and held the door open. Then Lucas got out, slowly and stiffly, exactly like a man who has spent the night chained to a bedpost....[T]he face was not even looking at them but just toward them, arrogant and calm with no more defiance in it than fear: detached, impersonal, almost musing, intractable and composed... (p. 44)
>
> [Lawyer Gavin Stevens to Lucas in the prison cell:] "Tell me exactly what happened yesterday." For another moment, Lucas didn't answer, sitting on the bunk, his hands on his knees, intractable and composed... (p. 61)
>
> [After Lucas's innocence has been proven, he insists on paying Gavin as the novel concludes, although it was not really the

lawyer whose work exonerated him:] So Lucas unknotted the sack and dumped the pennies out on the desk and counted them one by one moving each one with his forefinger into the first small mass of dimes and nickels, counting aloud, then snapped the purse shut…and wiped his hands and put the handkerchief back and stood again intractable and calm and not looking at either of them. (pp. 246–47)

Gavin Stevens—Faulkner's favorite lawyer over the course of many stories[8]—*is* paid, but three outsiders besides Lucas himself have really done the work. One is Gavin's nephew and the story's narrator, Chick. The adolescent's *narrative* "rigidity" in using words like "intractable" and "inflexible" time and again about Lukas is matched as the tale proceeds by his insistence on doing the right thing and digging up a white man's body in the very heart of redneck country. Yet, like Glaspell's outsider flexiphobes, he needs the support of others. Chick realizes that he cannot count on a mainstream lawyer, even a good one like his Uncle Gavin: they just think too flexibly; the lawyer's habit is to go by what Faulkner's narrator here calls "the rules and the cases." This has its excellent features, but its blindness to a more profound underlying reality becomes fatal, as we have seen in the response to Hitler from the Reich westward to Vichy and the British Channel Islands.

Lucas, like an excellent basketball coach facing a schedule of superstar opponents, gathers a team of non-mainstream players, of which Chick is the point guard. Chick is immeasurably assisted by his black boyhood friend, Aleck Sander, and an "old woman," the highly principled Miss Habersham. They will dig up the body of the victim alleged to be Lucas's and discover that the bullet could not have been fired from Lucas's gun.

As an outsider, Lucas Beauchamp can rely only on his steadfastness. He does better than another utterly inflexible outsider, the Jew Shylock.[9] But both racially persecuted literary figures display a flexiphobia born of long habit with majority communities that want to destroy them. Lucas's good luck, along with Minnie Foster's in "A Jury of Her Peers," is that he can find, where Shylock never does, flexiphobic allies in a just cause,

Notes

1. *Hamlet*, Hardin Craig and David Bevington, eds., *The Complete Works of Shakespeare* (Glenview, IL: Scott Foresman, 1973).

2. See my *"Hamlet* and Ressentiment," *American Imago* 29 (1972): 318.

3. First published as a short story in 1917, Glaspell's tale originated several years before as a theater piece called *Trifles,* first performed at the Provincetown Playhouse.

4. *Bradwell v. Illinois,* 16 Wall (83 US) 130 (1873).

5. *Hossack v. State*, 116 Iowa 194, 89 NW 1077 (Sup. Ct., Iowa, 1902).

6. *Bradwell v. Illinois*, concurring opinion of Justice Bradley. See also ch. 6, text at note 10.

7. William Faulkner, *Intruder in the Dust* (New York: Vintage, 1996; first published 1948). Bracketed page references are to the Vintage pocketbook edition.

8. See Richard Weisberg, "The Quest for Silence: Faulkner's Lawyer in a Comparative Setting," *Mississippi College Law Review* 4 (1984): 193.

9. For my approach to Shylock as beleaguered victim of Christian interpretive distortion in the trial scene, see Weisberg, " 'Then You Shall Be His Surety': Oaths and Mediating Breaches in *The Merchant of Venice*," in *Poethics and Other Strategies of Law and Literature* (New York: Columbia University Press, 1992), 94–104. See also this book, ch. 3, note 35.

6

Flexible Distortions of American Law, or How St. Paul and St. John Influence Fundamental Social Policy

a. Preserving the Possibility of Laudable Change within Interpretive Limits: Gradual Restoration of Five Flexible Misreadings of the US Constitution

As Sanford Levinson has shown to excellent effect, for many Americans these days the "sacred story" is neither biblical nor literary: it is the US Constitution.[1] Arguments about how to interpret it have struck remarkable parallels to biblical interpretation and have sometimes been just as contentious.[2] Lively debates have generated dubious theories in both fields, too. In constitutional law, we are inclined to contrast "originalists" to "living constitutionalists." Red-staters and/or constitutional theorists of a conservative stripe speak admiringly of "strict constructionists," those who (pre)tend to stick to text and original intention, which are somehow to be found in the sacred constitutive texts as written and ratified, decades and even centuries ago. On the other hand, "loose interpreters," if they are sitting judges, are accused of being "activists." Meanwhile, liberal theorists and most blue-staters pin the charge of "inflexibility" on the originalists, finding them insufficiently open to a "living Constitution," which has never been better defined than by the late Justice William Brennan in a 1986 essay:

We current justices read the Constitution in the only way we can: as twentieth-century Americans. We look to the history of the time of framing, and to the intervening history of interpretation. But the ultimate question must be: What do the words of the text mean for our time? For the genius of the Constitution rests not in any static meaning it might have had in a world that is dead and gone, but in the adaptability of the great principles to cope with current problems and current needs.[3]

I have always admired Justice Brennan's willingness to admit to a practice that evokes, at least for me, the interpretive technique of St. Paul and St. John. Perhaps it is not coincidental that this highly liberal and rightly admired participant in the equally rightly admired Warren Court's "activism" during the 1960s was raised as a Catholic. It does take an almost Jesuitical skill—and a small dose of chutzpah as well—to unanchor a sacred text from what *appeared* to have been (emphasis intended, as we shall see!) established meanings and to move instead to some inner voice that can "cope" with the new and the different. But my admiration for the Warren Court and this distinguished (Catholic) member derives from what I shall demonstrate here: that Court, which gave us *Brown v. Board of Education*, was primarily in the business of *restoring*, not "creating" meanings.

Still, what would our constitutional world look like, you might ask, if we did not have our judicial "activists" and if our Supreme Court did not occasionally play fast and loose with earlier authoritative interpretations? Haven't we needed precisely the St. Pauls and the St. Johns who were ready to overtake the Pharisaic insistence on "original meanings"?[4] Secular skepticism about what I am calling flexiphobia may reach its apex when we consider a constitutional world largely, much less exclusively, peopled by the "strict constructionists." "Separate but equal" might still be good law, and Faulkner's Jim Crow world (discussed in my previous chapter) might endure, with its lynchings, its "colored water fountains," and its segregated schools. Medieval methods of torture (another topic sadly requiring discussion in these pages) might be used to execute people. A woman's right to choose might not be protected.[5] The clock might be rolled back to where the tea party's kind of justice would proscribe even a married couple's use of contraception, and so on.

Self-identifying long ago with "moderate originalism,"[6] I want to show in that tradition how a reverence for text and the Framers' intentions does not contradict moving the Constitution forward into the generations that must live with it through new challenges and new technologies. I add to and to some extent reverse the usual account of how four constitutional amendments, construed in five actual cases perused in this chapter, have been interpreted. In many cases, especially those dealing with the "equal protection clause," analysts tend to conclude that only a malleable, nonoriginalist Supreme Court could progress from moves made by conservative justices and in so doing situate those amendments in the twentieth or twenty-first centuries. The more recent "correction" has been described, and either condemned or praised, as judicial "activism" unbound to text or intention. I claim, instead, that "loose" departures from text and tradition *brought about* anti-progressive and anti-textualist doctrine and then required decades of hard work to *restore* what should have been the original meaning. "Looseness" or even sometimes "living constitutionalism" unanchored from origins would not have been necessary if influential earlier justices had not already *flexibly* deformed original meanings in decisions that then either had to be overturned or are still out there needing restorative work. My most salient example of the latter distortion involves the Second Amendment, and the current Supreme Court's St. Paul-like ability to find within that resisting text an individual right to own guns.

The first interpretive shot taken by the Supreme Court at the featured four amendments missed the mark because of creative distortions of one kind or another. To that extent, the justices behaved like the early Jesus movement writers we have discussed. They let their excessive and unlikely vision overwhelm a fair reading of the texts in question. And, like the early Christian writers, they achieved successes that, although holding out considerable attraction to various audiences, have proven deleterious, and sometimes tragically harmful.

I need to set the table for my arguments here by insisting that my readers take a vow, a kind of "credo." You must accept going in that the Constitution is an enduringly useful and occasionally inspiring structuring document, even as we the people move chronologically away from its founding and into this second decade of the twenty-first century. Perhaps exemplifying Professor Levinson's "constitutional faith,"[7] and as one who has taught constitutional law for almost four decades (fully 15 percent of the time the text has been in existence!), I remain a true believer.

Once that vow is taken, through an act of reason or faith or some combination of both, I ask you to adopt two corollaries. First, consider that constitutional interpretation can be split along religious lines, too. Professor Levinson offers helpfully his sectarian equivalent of the "strict/loose" or "passive/activist" dichotomies: for a "Protestant" kind of reader of sacred texts, deviations from the original sense of the sacred document need to be justified, particularly since authoritative interpreters such as Supreme Court justices (or Popish prelates) need never face the people their decisions affect. Conversely, though, there is a "Catholic" way of interpreting the Constitution. As my entire book has argued, thanks to Sts. Paul, John, and others such as St. Peter, some readers (like Justice Brennan, perhaps) may have opted into that tradition, one that *authorizes departures* from literal text or likely intention: a priestly class, usually unelected, gets to decide according to its own often unstated premises what a text means.[8]

My second corollary is fully secular, and I mentioned a version of it in Chapter 2 in the discussion of Gutmann and Thompson's recent book on compromise: it involves a distinction between "rules," which are fairly absolute, and "principles," which more flexibly guide judges to what they think of as the right answer, and we owe the version of it I use here to the great legal philosopher, Ronald Dworkin.[9] *Rules*, although of course subject to some "furry edges" as the positivist H. L. A. Hart called them, generally ask for "a single fundamental test for law," whereas *principles* often involve a call to decision making based on factors that are not necessarily based on written law or precedent. Two familiar examples should be reiterated here.

First, the women in "A Jury of Her Peers," you may recall, continued to suffer from the invocation of an anti-feminist *principle* emphasized by the Supreme Court decades earlier. In lieu of adopting the *rule* given by the literal text of the Fourteenth Amendment, providing the equal protection of the laws, Supreme Court Justice Bradley opted for a more flexible guiding idea: he pulled the "woman's place is in the home" dogma out of his hat and helped stop lawyer Myra Bradwell from joining the Illinois Bar.[10]

Second, the Catholic Church in Hitler's Europe explicitly avoided its own strict rules against racism and advised the Vichy government it could proceed to legislate against the Jews according to the more flexible *principle* of realpolitik.

Whatever the vocabulary, religious or secular, I challenge the simplistic supposition that only "flexibly creative [read: rule-skeptical, or 'Catholic']" interpretations, which seem to defy the original sense of the constitutional text, take us to where we need to be to substantiate our present faith in that document, as well as in certain traditions flowing from it such as a taboo on torture. In other words, and I am hardly the first to say this, the opposition of "strict" to "loose" constructionists of the Constitution is misleading, particularly if it entails the equation "strict = non-activist = conservative" while "loose = activist = progressive" and especially if we add to that bipolar approach that strict constructionists show their stripes by keeping themselves within the bounds of "originalism" while loose constructionists show their "living constitutional" colors by liberating themselves from any attention to what white men hundreds of years ago might have written or wanted. The dichotomy appeals to political discourse and has also been extended to the conservatives wanting the judge to be an "impartial umpire" while the blue-staters do not usually mind her occasionally "making law."

As Stanley Fish put it awhile ago of "the oft-opposed policies of judicial restraint and judicial activism":

> It is often assumed that the one indicates a respect for the Constitution while the other is an unwarranted exercise of interpretive power, as influenced by social and political views; but in fact, so-called judicial restraint is exercised by those judges who, for a variety of reasons, decide to leave in place the socially and politically based interpretations of the activists of an earlier generation.[11]

This chapter is all about those earlier "activist" Supreme Court justices, some now considered liberal and others conservative, who commandeered a constitutional text not previously interpreted (or at least not authoritatively) and who erred badly in moving way beyond the text, or even contradicting it, so that in some cases others over long periods of time had to fight hard to *restore* rather than change appropriate meanings. They are, in the terms of this book, the Sts. Paul and John of textual interpretation, the infinitely flexible ones needing correction over time through the restorative work of lawyers and ordinary citizens.

I begin in this chapter with a case that came down some three decades after the unfortunate would-be practitioner Myra Bradwell saw shot down her straightforward claim that the relatively new Equal Protection Clause of the Fourteenth Amendment vouchsafed her a place in the exclusive male conclave of the Illinois Bar Association. In *Hans v. Louisiana* (1890), the same Justice Bradley who relegated Myra to the kitchen restated the text of the Eleventh Amendment in a bizarre way, setting in motion problems that are still being worked through. I continue with *Plessy v. Ferguson* (1896), *Schenck v. the United States* (1919), *Everson v. NJ* (1947), and *DC v. Heller* (2008). In all five cases, the Supreme Court mismanaged the constitutional text because the justices were acting *flexibly*, not narrowly, and their decisions forced and are forcing the steadfast to back and fill to *restore* deliberately abandoned meanings.

I. In *Hans v. Louisiana* (1890),[12] the text of the Eleventh Amendment, ratified in 1798, reads as follows:

> The Judicial power of the United States shall not be construed to extend to any suit in law or equity, commenced or prosecuted against one of the United States by Citizens of another State, or by Citizens or Subjects of any Foreign State.

Undoubtedly less familiar to my readers than the rest of this quintet of unfortunate Supreme Court decisions, *Hans* took up the Eleventh Amendment 92 years after it was ratified. The Court changed its meaning while purporting to preserve it or, in our terms here, it "pulled a St. Paul" on the older text. Instead of merely limiting federal court claims against states by out-of-staters or foreigners, *Hans* went much further and granted the states immunity from suits brought by its *own* citizens against it. Constitutional scholar Jack Balkin describes the admittedly complicated outgrowth of the Court's betrayal of plain meaning in blessedly simple terms:

> *Hans*...seems to be inconsistent with the constitutional text....Current doctrine reads "citizens of another state" to include citizens of the same state [cite omitted] and also allows suits in equity through the fiction of suits against the state's attorney general [cite omitted]. Perhaps the best defense of some kind of state immunity is a structural argument for protection of state sovereignty under the Tenth Amendment [cite omitted], but it is not at all clear why structural considerations should produce the doctrine we currently have.[13]

The astounding leap in *Hans* from the text purported, but erroneously, to reinstate a better "policy" that it claimed had prevailed prior to the adoption of the Eleventh Amendment, where even a state's own citizens could not sue it in federal court. But the *Hans* court's sense of history was skewed, and it got its facts wrong. Purporting to show that feudal lords, the equivalent, say, of our states, could not be sued in their own courts by their tenants, the equivalent of a state's citizens, the *Hans* decision largely ignored the historical fact that the landlords *could* be sued in the king's courts, the equivalent of the federal court jurisdiction provided for a state's own citizens against a state by the literal text of the Eleventh Amendment.[14]

I have been arguing that there is a questionable pedigree going back to the early Jesus movement for such "wide ranging"[15] interpretive practices, and I shall proceed to show now that these practices needlessly delayed the implementation of sound policies that should have derived almost directly from the text and history of other better-known amendments; instead, as with

Justice Bradley instructing Ms. Bradwell that her place was in the home, "wide ranging" departures from text occasioned disastrous doctrine that then required patchwork sweat and commitment to overturn. The creative misreading of the Eleventh Amendment by the *Hans v. Louisiana* justices has required restorative correction by later Supreme Courts, including especially those sitting on the "activist" Court that brought us (as we shall see) *Brown v. Board of Education*. After some hard work, those justices found implied waivers by states to the immunity that *Hans* had granted them without any textual or historical support.[16]

We now find the same structure of restoration as we move to the more familiar language of the Fourteenth Amendment. In the immediate post–Civil War period, an "equal protection" clause was added, and for the first time equality became a bedrock principle in the US Constitution. How firm was that bedrock, however, when justices such as Bradley, whom we have situated against the text when Myra Bradwell sought admission to the all-male Illinois bar, took their double-edged axe to it?

II. In *Plessy* (1896),[17] that same Equal Protection Clause that Justice Bradley mangled was distorted when the Supreme Court voted to permit "separate but equal" public facilities. Looking at the Fourteenth Amendment's text "No state shall … deny to any person within its jurisdiction the equal protection of the laws," the Court had a choice, and it made the wrong one. *Plessy* began by distorting or ignoring some important case-specific facts; under the challenged Louisiana statute, Homer Plessy had been removed from a "whites only" railroad car because he was one-eighth "colored," but the Court did not take notice of the fact that no white person voluntarily sitting in a "colored" car would have been similarly forced to move. Conversely, "colored" nannies were exempted from the separation if they were tending to white babies. Factual omissions and distortions are hardly unique to

Plessy's interpretive methodology, and, as we saw when the early Jesus movement benefited from mistranslations and historical manipulation, they assist in producing unfortunate doctrine. In effect, *Plessy* bypassed the conclusion that the railroad's racial policies and its facilities were not really "separate" and most probably not "equal" either. It found that the equal protection clause was satisfied by state and local laws that separated the races in public facilities.

The factual predicate of separate but equal was already false, and the Court launched decades of suffering under "Jim Crow." A less flexible analysis of the mere wording of the Fourteenth Amendment should have avoided altogether the far less rule-based result unfortunately reached in *Plessy*. Instead, with only Justice Harlan in dissent, the Court said:

> The object of the [Fourteenth] Amendment was undoubtedly to enforce the absolute equality of the two races before the law, but in *the nature of things* it could not have been intended to abolish distinctions based upon color, or to enforce social, as distinguished from political, equality, or a commingling of the two races upon terms *unsatisfactory to either*. Laws permitting, and even requiring their separation in places where they are liable to be brought into contact do not *necessarily* imply the inferiority of either race to the other. [emphasis added]

The text of the Fourteenth Amendment, read faithfully, might better have been interpreted to strike down a statute such as Lousiana's, which provided a spurious equality through separation. The slippery work of going the opposite way depended on phrases such as the ones I have emphasized. The Court takes it upon itself to figure out the Amendment using vaguely articulated principles of its own, perhaps racism itself, unarticulated premises divorced from the rule it could have crafted from the text itself.

Separation does not "necessarily" mean inequality, the Court says disingenuously. But if it *might* mean that to a recently freed person of color, should not the segregationist policy yield to the constitutional text? The majority's vague phrase "the nature of things" indicates that—not for the last time in history[18]—socially significant meanings would be derived from the "spirit" of a text, something to be found inside the justices subjectively, and not from the textual meaning itself or the probable intentions of those who wrote and ratified it.

The phrase "equal protection of the laws," as lone dissenter John Marshall Harlan stated, means that no one, under law, gets kicked out of anywhere by anyone just because of his or her race. And this is especially true given that the Fourteenth Amendment was *intended* for the benefit of the newly freed slaves against the oppression of such states as Louisiana. So, for Harlan, dissenting in *Plessy*, there was this flexiphobic reality:

> In respect of civil rights, all citizens are equal before the law. [This decision will] defeat the beneficent purposes which the people of the United States had in view when they adopted the recent amendments of the Constitution.[19]

As usual, prophetic voices call on colleagues to redeem textual meaning rather than to stray from it! How much intransigent work then became necessary to restore, for black people and then for women, and then for gays and lesbians, meanings that already inhered in the text being interpreted!

The difficult path to a restoration of Harlan's righteous truth has been told and retold, and it is especially inspiring when it emphasizes the hard work of stubborn lawyers like Thurgood

Marshall, who toiled tirelessly to end "separate but equal,"[20] and of lower federal court judges in the South who intransigently brought about changes on the ground in the face of stiff resistance.[21]

To many, the 1954 decision in *Brown v. Board* proved that "strict" readings of the Constitution stood in the way of progress and that correct outcomes flowed from flexible readings unanchored to text or history. To others, like my favorite law professor Herbert Wechsler, *Brown* erred, not because of its holding but rather because its reasoning violated what he famously called "neutral principles."[22] He worried because he saw an insufficient analytical basis on which to depart from *Plessy,* the operative case in point.

Both sides in that debate avoided a simpler analysis, one that would fully celebrate at least the apartheid-destroying outcome in *Brown* while decidedly not concluding that the Court violated ensconced and neutral methods of reading the Constitution and precedent! *Brown* was not a flexible departure from text, *but a return to it.* Its "neutral principle" was the restoration of the proper rule that was always already to be found in the Fourteenth Amendment. Had less flexible justices in *Plessy* resolved this case textually at the outset, then *Brown* would not have been necessary. The happy turn in 1954 was not toward judicial anarchy but rather *back* to text and intent, not toward infinite judicial flexibility but rather *toward* intractability.

III., IV. *Schenck* (1919) and *Everson* (1947), two cases construing the First Amendment, demonstrate similar problems caused by excessively flexible authoritative misreadings requiring decades of still ongoing restorative improvement. *Schenck v. United States*[23] and *Everson v. NJ*[24] construed the highlighted sections of that well-known font of American liberty:

Amendment I. (1791). Congress shall make no law *respecting an establishment of religion*, or prohibiting the free exercise thereof; or *abridging the freedom of speech*, or of the press; or the right of the people peaceably to assemble, and to petition the Government for redress of grievances.

Schenck had been arrested under a federal, World War I–era sedition law rendering criminal his written statements in opposition to the war effort. Didn't this text protect him from punishment? What could be more simple for the interpreter? Just as Isaiah means what he says and not some deep foreshadowing of an individual life 800 years after he wrote, so the Framers meant "no law." Even if some speech acts were obviously not given this blanket protection from potential criminal liability—fraud, for example—*political speech* such as Schenck's lay at the most protected core of the amendment, whose whole idea is to shield unpopular dissenting speech from the federal government's powerful censoring hand.

Unpredictably, given the First Amendment, but predictably when we recall the centuries of textual deformation during "emergencies," Schenck's prison sentence was upheld. In the process of rationalizing such a flexible departure from the text and intentions of the Framers, Justice Oliver Wendell Holmes stated that the First Amendment would not protect someone "shouting fire falsely in a crowded theater." If the government can punish such a speech act, concluded this oracular justice—thrice wounded in the Civil War and the Delphic oracle of all judges—it can surely punish Schenck, whose pamphlets caused a "clear and present danger" of harms Congress had the right to enjoin.

Just as the early Jesus movement's interpretations of the Bible eventually won the hearts of billions of people, Holmes's rhetorical invocation of an "emergency" has had great rhetorical appeal. His authoritative drift, from the First Amendment's rule to a lesser untextual principle of panic in a crisis, has had enormous appeal.

Think about it twice, however: first, *do* most people respond to mere speech at their peril—say, trampling each other on their way to the exits—without first corroborating the screaming hypothetical liar's remark? When you hear a fire alarm go off at work, what is your reaction? When an evangelist shouts at you "The world is at an end!" what do you do? If they tell you to jump off the Brooklyn Bridge, do you do so? As I have written elsewhere, the Framers were deeply skeptical about the power of mere words to cause people to act when they otherwise would not; they thought of language as "a cloudy medium,"[25] puny compared to other human impulses and activities. They felt that governments would do less well in censoring, than in permitting, protests and other forms of mere speech. If you do not allow a pamphlet, or even an occasional "leakage" of information through truthful discourse, worse will happen when more violent means of opposing governments arise because the "cloudy medium" of speech had been suppressed. Holmes violates this basic, originalist grounding of the First Amendment.

Then, too, what does the crowded theater example have to do with Schenck's political opposition to World War I? He was speaking not in crowded places but before recruits who were pretty much in the process of conscription and had no reason whatsoever to read his opinions. (No conscript changed his mind because of Schenck's words.) So to get from here to there, Holmes dexterously joined the theater hypothetical to the appealing phrase "clear and present danger" that formed the judgment's legal standard. If political protest stood some chance of causing some of those recruits to decline to be drafted, the Court held—thus diminishing the First Amendment—the speech would not be protected.

A flexiphobic approach to the First Amendment would have declined to bend law away from the text's powerful constraint on government punishment of speech. It took years of work analogous to those of *Plessy* through *Brown*, to get things back to the original idea of the First Amendment.[26] Repentant, however, Justice Holmes himself, under the influence of Justice Brandeis and Judge Learned Hand, flip-flopped quickly. He reversed his own position and began protecting political protest, albeit usually in dissent from his original flexible misstep.[27] *Too little, too late.* The later Holmes/Brandeis dissents did nothing to undo the convictions of subsequent political protesters, presidential candidates, anarchists, Marxists, and pamphleteers of all stripes whose words could be shoehorned by government into the one-size-fits-all parameters of the "clear and present danger test." Original wisdom reemerged only in 1969, *Brandenburg v. Ohio*, when the overly flexible and hence dangerous "clear and present danger test" was rigorously restricted to speech acts that were both "directed to inciting or producing imminently lawless action and...likely to incite or produce such action."[28] Even shouting fire falsely in a crowded theater—much less distributing political pamphlets or advocating in classrooms the violent overthrow of government—no longer fell into this narrow exception to First Amendment protections.

IV. One of the First Amendment's other clauses received, similarly, an errant authoritative reading in a 1947 case in which the relationship of church and state was first fully tested in the Supreme Court. In *Everson*, some New Jersey taxpayers objected to having to subsidize public transportation for Catholic schoolchildren to and from parochial schools. They invoked the "establishment clause," which is far less transparent in its meaning than the "speech clause" Justice Holmes managed to avoid in a slippery fashion in *Schenck*.

In a somewhat bizarre result, the Court permitted the state to impose what amounted to a tax in support of religious education. The establishment clause, if it means anything at all, was designed, precisely, to avoid the ills that confronted the colonists, who recalled the experience in England of an established church and who—although like Americans today, often quite religious[29]—disliked the practice and wanted church and state to be separated. At the time, both secularists like Thomas Jefferson and religious leaders such as Roger Williams advocated what each from his different standpoint called "a wall of separation,"[30] which from either perspective would have tried to avoid imposing support for religion from the state's fiscal coffers. Strangely, *Everson's* rhetoric everywhere reflected endorsement of that metaphor, particularly where it came to assessing a financial imposition on taxpayers to subsidize religious practices, the very ill the First Amendment was designed to cure:

> The "establishment of religion" clause of the First Amendment means at least this: Neither a state nor the Federal Government can set up a church. Neither can pass laws which aid one religion, aid all religions, or prefer one religion over another. Neither can force nor influence a person to go to or remain away from church against his will or force him to profess a belief or disbelief in any religion.... No tax in any amount, large or small, can be levied to support any religious activities or institutions, whatever they may be called, or whatever form they may adopt to teach or practice religion.... In the words of Jefferson, the clause against establishment of religion was intended to create "a wall of separation between church and State."

We are learning that the terms "strict" and "loose" construction of the Constitution—and their parallels, "cautious" and "activist" justices—can be deceptive, and that the concept of intransigence helps untie various knotty contradictions when we use those tag-words. In *Everson*, "strict" construction of the Constitution would have nipped in the bud the possibility of severe breaches in the "wall of separation" between church and state. The authority of the text and the Framers stood mutually opposed to a fiscal subvention of these students' carfare to and from their parochial schools.

Despite its own strong rhetoric, however, the *Everson* majority upheld the legislation in favor of the Catholic Church. Bus fare to and from sectarian school is a pittance, but requiring a secular taxpayer to subvent it is an enormity.

We are still fighting this fight. No recent justice was more alert to the strange quality of *Everson*—which remains persuasive authority—than Sandra Day O'Connor. In a 1995 case testing whether Jefferson's university down in Virginia could deny a student fee's being allocated to an evangelical publication, O'Connor voted to force the public university to pay the religious publication's expenses, despite the Establishment Clause. She was conflicted, but *Everson* gave her solace:

> *Everson* provided perhaps the strongest exposition of the no-funding principle: "No tax in any amount, large or small, can be levied to support any religious activity."...Yet the Court approved the use of public funds, in a general program, to reimburse parents for their children's bus fares to attend Catholic schools. Although some would cynically dismiss the Court's disposition as being inconsistent with its protestations [she cites Justice Jackson in dissent to *Everson:* "the most fitting precedent is that of Julia who, according to Byron's reports, 'whispering "I will ne'er consent," consented'"], the decision reflected the need to rely on careful judgment—not simple categories—when two principles

of equal historical and jurisprudential pedigree, come into unavoidable conflict.[31]

Simplicity again yielded to the lure of conflicting principles. Yes, the Christian student publishers surely also had rights of free speech against the government-sponsored university. Justice O'Connor realized full well that if funding them violated the Establishment Clause, the students' rights would have to yield to the embedded rule; Everson's confusing outcome gave her, and the Court, a way to permit a public university to underwrite an evangelical student newspaper.

Our First Amendment jurisprudence regarding church and state is by now confusing; in fact, it is "in shambles," as described by Justice Clarence Thomas, who has contributed to the confusion on a basic level.[32] *Everson* added in full measure, through its slippery avoidance of its own steadfast rhetoric, to the flexible mess.

Indeed, when authoritative Courts plunder the texts and flexibly deform original meanings, they force later advocates and justices to deal with their error and return to rightness. Meanwhile, much suffering over long periods of time ensues.

V. And this brings us to *DC v Heller*,[33] a case decided in 2008 by the current Supreme Court's most outspoken "textualist," Justice Antonin Scalia. In a recent book about legal interpretation, the justice and his co-author Bryan Garner "seek to restore [!] sound interpretive conventions.... [Yet Scalia] does not swear that the opinions he joins or writes in the future will comply with what is written here."[34] He confesses immediately that the strict textualism his book espouses will yield where necessary and for reasons left unstated to the more elastic needs of twenty-first-century America. Thus does the current Court's loudest proponent of "originalism" show his stripes. What a "restoration"! Sounding very much like the Catholic Church's position to

Vichy—we believe in one thing but will adjust that belief almost infinitely when it is called into question[35]—Justice Scalia propounds the faith of looking only to the text as it would have been understood at the time of its framing but then guarantees that he will breach the faith whenever convenience so dictates. Not for the first time,[36] Scalia in *Heller* manages to avoid his own so-called "strictness" and to maneuver the constitutional text in a manner that would have pleased those decided "loose constructionists" of the early Christian movement.

Heller provided Scalia, as it had Justices Bradley and Holmes before him, an opportunity to construe one of the Bill of Rights that had not as yet been authoritatively interpreted.

The Second Amendment says:

> A well-regulated Militia, being necessary to the security of a free State, the right of the people to keep and bear Arms, shall not be infringed.

In *Heller*, a majority of the Court found, through this text, that we all have been given an *individual* right to bear arms. Arguably, the plain meaning of the twenty-six words of the amendment, together with its syntax, speaks of safeguarding the *state's* right to have an armed militia. As two vigorous dissents (by Justices Stevens and Breyer) elaborate convincingly, with the help of a compendious *amicus* brief to the Court by several professors of literature and linguistics,[37] the first twelve words seem to limit the last fourteen, so that the Framers appear to encourage state militia checks on potential national despots. They do not speak to a personal right to keep guns or any firearms for purposes of self-defense or for hunting or to impress one's neighbors.

Justice Scalia, in a sixty-four-page decision that is far less a model of clarity than the amendment he so throws into ambiguity, manages to do away almost entirely with the words of what he labels the "prefatory clause," focusing instead on the "operative clause" and more or less dissociating the clauses altogether. But since the phrase "keep and bear arms" all by itself hardly shows that possessing handguns for self-defense was to be protected, Scalia needed to be nimble even regarding the "operative phrase" standing alone. "Keep" seems at first blush to set up a condition precedent for the act of bearing (or using) arms; if that is true, then the right again applies to ensuring a readiness for armed conflict of the type embodied in the idiom "bear arms against," that is warfare and not self-defense or hunting or anything else.

The "textualist" half of originalism, the only one Scalia ostensibly values, has proven elusive if you need to show that those twenty-six words are speaking of an individual right to bear arms. The other "originalist" anchor, the Framers' intention, is usually disdained by Scalia as impossible to find and almost always indeterminate,[38] but he is forced by circumstances here to try to answer Justice Stevens's dissent finding that early American history situates the right to bear arms in militias and not in personal self-defense. The Framers had in mind here a state of readiness against the threat of tyrannical national power. By insisting that a group of men in each state be allowed to "keep" arms, they forged a compromise—not one that Avishai Margalit would have labeled "rotten"[39]—with their anti-Federalist colleagues who distrusted national power. As Scalia feels duty bound to report: "Petitioners point to militia laws of the founding period that required militia members to 'keep' arms in connection with militia service, and they conclude from this that the phrase 'keep arms' has a militia-related connotation." Later, though—role playing perhaps as a latter day St. John—Scalia ridicules this plausible reading and the intransigent dissenting justices who propound it:

[T]hey manufacture a hybrid definition, whereby "bear arms" connotes the actual carrying of arms (and therefore is not really an idiom) but only in the service of an organized militia [so that]...the phrase "keep and bear Arms" would be incoherent. The word "Arms" would have two different meanings at once: "weapons" (as the object of "keep") and (as the object of "bear") one-half of an idiom ["bear arms against"]. It would be rather like saying "He filled and kicked the bucket" to mean "He filled the bucket and died." Grotesque.

Yes, we might agree, this is "grotesque," but we would be pointing to Scalia's words and not his opponents'. Or maybe he is being just "too clever by a half,"[40] or—more seriously, because we have seen such interpretive maneuvering before in the pages of this book—he may be engaging in a kind of lie-against-the text where any means to the end of a desired outcome is permitted. He cannot deny that "keep and bear" forms a totally coherent compound phrase, so he insists that "bear Arms" can only mean "wage warfare" if it is followed by the word "against." As finicky and imprecise as that move is, it fails anyway when we return, as we must, to the prefatory twelve words: for if I say, somewhat analogously to the Second Amendment, "Today being a fine day, I shall prepare and eat a picnic," I mean to join as a condition precedent the excellence of the weather to my planned compound activity. When the weather turns bad, I shall no longer want my picnic; when the need for a militia is excised, the right to keep and bear arms—for any reason—is attenuated.

The common wisdom is that only flexible, or "activist" courts, unanchored to original traditions and meanings, can keep our Constitution relevant to new times. In fact, the progressions I have indicated here show that problems arise when plain meanings and (more complicated) intentions are betrayed by authoritative justices writing *flexibly,* instead of faithfully, on clean slates that later have to be recleansed and restored by flexiphobic successor Courts.

b. The Violation of Legal Taboos in the Wake of an "Emergency": The Aftermath of 9/11

Starting immediately after September 11, 2001, the United States and many "blue-state" policy makers and academics began compromising texts and traditions that were understood beforehand as precious; they were not necessarily constitutional in origin, but they involved well-preserved understandings of what America does not do, even in the face of an "emergency," such as condone torture, extreme rendition, near-limitless detention of prisoners, extensive warrantless eavesdropping, violations of lawyer-client protections, unilateral decisions to target individuals for drone killings.

In the first comprehensive book-length study of the nation's response to post-9/11 practices, I labeled as "loose professionalism" the already evident capacity of many American lawyers to compromise these traditions.[41] Flexible thinking was rampant, as those charged with safeguarding basic American traditions of law pulled their own imitations of Sts. Paul and John on previous understandings.

As David K. Shipler puts it recently in his *Rights of the People*:

> If [our] rights were solid, all of the people's stories would be uplifting. But parts of the Bill of Rights are eroding— dramatically in the war on terrorism.[42]

As this book goes to press, there is some reason to feel that opinion makers on the left who had not paid that much attention to aberrational practices for a while are now trying to correct them. The Senate, in fits and starts and often responding to some "red-state" filibusters,[43] holds hearings on such newer variations as drone killings. Even Guantanamo and its excesses draw fire. At the same time, we are told that most Americans cannot get very excited about these issues[44]—perhaps having been conditioned over a dozen years and two otherwise diametrically opposed presidencies to accept them.

I offer an account of a domestic process of accommodation, a contemporary snapshot within the millennia-long montage, which was created by St. Paul and came into modern focus with the flexible Enlightenment. The emergency instantiated by 9/11 engendered, almost predictably, the high degree of inaccuracy and equivocation that has characterized so much policy and practice over the centuries.

The story begins on September 10, 2001. No one—or very few who had any influence—would have entertained that day the briefest suggestion that torture would be tolerated as an official practice; that suspects could be incarcerated without trial in American-controlled prisons for indefinite and indeed limitless periods; that special courts using procedures associated with martial law would take control even over civilian defendants and even when regular courts and judges bound by safeguards were open and functioning; that the Fourth Amendment's proscription on "unreasonable searches and seizures" would be found to permit tracking Americans through their cell phones or eavesdropping on them without judicial warrant; or that the executive power ought to include targeting citizens for execution by drone missile prior to any arrest or trial.

In the blinking of an eye, these taboos became negotiable. Just as Vichy lawyers trained in egalitarianism folded in the face of a discourse that traded "emergency" for lawful tradition,

American modes of reasoning readapted the 2,000-year-old habit of distorting ensconced and worthy understandings so that, without sound means, ends desperately craved might be achieved.

At first the diminishing ranks of post 9/11 flexiphobes sought consolation—as had Jacques Maury, Abraham Lainé, and Judge Lothar Kreyssig—in the thought that their previously like-minded colleagues and friends would again see clearly a few respectful months or so after the fall of the World Trade Center towers. As time went on and things got worse, they still managed to preserve the hope that a change in administration would restore (as newer Supreme Courts had done by correcting the flexible errors of *Plessy*, *Schenck*, and such other interpretive aberrations as *Bowers v. Hardwick*)[45] the deeply held understandings of constitutional rights.

But the steadfast few deceived themselves. Shipler (2011), writing three or more years into the Obama administration, observes:

> Obama's election in 2008 shook the kaleidoscope sharply but did not discard all pieces of the troubling pattern. His administration released documents on torture but withheld photographs of abuse in Abu Ghraib prison, transferred some terrorism suspects to criminal courts but reserved the option of indefinite detention, and continued widespread monitoring of Americans' communications. . . . It remains to be seen how history will judge the violations after September 11, and how lasting the legal corruptions in constitutional violations will be. . . . The decision will be favorable if we nurture our checks and balances, if we push back hard to maintain our constitutional liberties. (pp. 27, 33, 389)

Before any George W. Bush White House memoranda on the subject were widely distributed, law professors of some liberal distinction began playing around with torture as a potentially acceptable practice. You can do this, of course, while preserving an antipathy to torture. You can ratchet up the definition so that few interrogation practices any longer fall within it: "We don't do 'torture,' but lesser inhumane methods might be OK."[46] You can permit it but demand, as Alan Dershowitz did, some kind of secret judicial warrant so that players remained "accountable."[47] You can squeeze as much juice as possible out of "ticking bomb" hypotheticals.[48] You can morph from rigor to flexibility simply by admitting (often with tones of regret) that a "conversation" indeed had begun about what was hitherto taboo, so why not "listen to all arguments"? Your Vatican-like move from uncompromising "thesis" to infinitely malleable "hypothesis" can even lead you to dredge up years-old judicial decisions that you had abjured and somehow make them sound OK again: until 9/11, for example, no one would have dared reapprove the Supreme Court decisions, such as *Korematsu*,[49] which had permitted the enforced detention during World War II in west coast "camps" of thousands of loyal Japanese-Americans; even *Korematsu* was rescued from the garbage heap of Supreme Court mistakes. As the ship of flexibility moves from Enlightened responsiveness toward fatal redirection, any port in the storm is welcome, even those that had long before been avoided at all costs.

Fairly early in the game, Elaine Scarry and I were described by reviewers of a pioneering volume on the subject of post-9/11 practices as the only two—among a dozen or so contributors—who unequivocally opposed the progression toward torture or related techniques.[50] Of course, there were then and are to this day flexiphobic *defenders* of the new approach to 9/11 challenges. I welcomed their overt arguments for torture, wiretapping, and prolonged detention. One of this book's suggestions is that clear-cut opponents, unlike covert, secretive, or seemingly equivocal enemies, assist one side better to understand the other and to take action against it quicker, more communally, and more effectively. One of these worthy opponents—although one known to change his mind long after the fact—was Richard A. Posner, who defended the view that the Constitution is "not a suicide pact"[51] and hence needs the pliability to survive external threat.

Time, I believe, will prove Shipler's case to be stronger than Posner's. When we give up the ghost in the name of survival, we are either sacrificing everything worth preserving or—far more likely—we are grossly exaggerating the "emergency" that induces such abandonments. Time indeed always seems to teach us—with the exception of the Jesus movement emergency-inspired distortion, which still requires ongoing correction[52]—that we err when we let our darker angels budge us from the preservation of the good. Why can we not figure that out before we once again "go loose" on fine traditions?

Of course, I have argued that our opponents' overt dogmatism helps us precisely so that we can be inflexible in our resolve to overcome them. Are not torture and droning exactly the way to show our *inflexible resolve against terrorism*?

NO! Many indefinite detentions touch innocent people, as do drone attacks and widespread eavesdropping. Our traditions offer sound alternatives, even during perpetual states of "emergency," to draconian methods such as these.

Human nature does not inevitably lead to errant patterns of interpretation, understanding, and action. Something in the culture that need not always be our habit-of-choice has played a 2,000-year-old role. We can do better, but the behavior of the Executive Branch since 9/11 bids fair to bring infinite flexibility into its third millennium of mistakes.

b. Executive Branch Memoranda Writers Who Abuse Text and Tradition

1. The Yoo/Bybee Memos

On September 25, 2001, a man named John Yoo, then deputy assistant attorney general, wrote to President George W. Bush's deputy counsel a twenty-one-page memorandum[53] opining "as to the scope of the President's authority to take military action in response to the terrorist attacks [of 9/11]." Speaking to what Yoo called the "grave national emergency," the memo grapples with the long-standing tension—both constitutional and statutory—of sharing war-making power with Congress and concludes: "we think it beyond question that the President has the plenary constitutional power to take such military action as he deems necessary and appropriate.... Force can be used both to retaliate for those attacks, and to prevent and deter future attacks on the Nation" (p. 24). The following January 9, Yoo managed to conclude that "neither the federal War Crimes Act nor the Geneva Convention [including Common Articles 2 and 3] would apply to the detention conditions in Guantanamo Bay, Cuba, or to trial by military commission of al Qaeda or Taliban prisoners [and that...] customary international law has no binding legal effect on either the President or the military because it is not federal law, as recognized by the Constitution" (p. 79). On August 1, 2002, Yoo and Jay S. Bybee, then assistant attorney general of the United States, opined to then Attorney General Alberto R. Gonzalez in complementary memoranda that "the [George Walker] Bush administration's understanding created a valid and effective reservation to the Torture Convention. Even if it were otherwise, there is no international court to review the conduct of the United States under the Convention" (p. 220). Bybee, on that day, concluded both that several operative laws and treaties against the practice of torture were inapplicable to al Qaeda and its allies and that, anyway:

> [T]orture...covers only extreme acts. Severe pain is gener-
> ally of the kind difficult for the victim to endure. Where the
> pain is physical, it must be of an intensity akin to that which
> accompanies serious physical injury such as death or organ
> failure. (p. 213–14)

These memos played fast and loose with the Constitution, judicial decisions, international treaties, and customary law[54] and may have been based not on those long-standing precedents but on a then very recent thirty-seven-page instructional manual of seven techniques later incorporated into the memos.[55] Once a process of extreme departure begins, any straw will be grasped at to support a new set of destabilizing theories.

So it appeared to the more flexiphobic of contemporary observers—once the memos were released and they knew what they were dealing with—and so has concluded "history"; on February 19, 2010, the Justice Department released a series of confidential reports by the Office of Professional Responsibility about some of these memos that concluded that Yoo had "put his desire to accommodate the client [President Bush] above his obligation to provide thorough, objective and candid legal advice, and...therefore committed intentional professional misconduct."[56] Both Yoo and Bybee avoided professional discipline only because "one Justice Department official [David Margolis] over-ruled the OPR recommendation, although he said Yoo and Bybee 'had exercised "poor judgment"' [and he...] called the memos 'an unfortunate chapter in the history of the Office of Legal Counsel.'"[57]

Yoo and Bybee had issued forth the kind of "off the wall" reading of established texts that we have sourced here to the findings by brilliant men 2,000 years ago of types and predictions in older texts that could not bear such readings authentically. "Off the wall" interpretations that would not pass muster in secondary school classrooms squeezed through and became authoritative. As David Cole reports of the eventual critique of the torture memos, "*no one* who reviewed Yoo's work gave it a passing grade" (Emphasis in original):

> The OPR and Margolis largely agreed that Yoo's memos contained many serious flaws. Yoo interpreted the ban on torture to require the intentional infliction of severe pain on the level associated with death and organ failure, a standard he imported from a health benefits statute having no relevance to the issue at hand. The standard is literally meaningless, as neither death nor organ failure is associated with any particular level of pain. Some people die painlessly; others suffer extreme pain. The same holds true for organ failure. Yoo appears to have adopted this gloss not to clarify what is prohibited but to send the message that only an extraordinarily high degree of pain amounts to torture. Yoo also wrote that an interrogator could inflict even that level of pain so long as he did not "specifically intend" to do so.[58]

What Attorney General Michael Mukasey—Gonzalez's replacement late in the game—called a "slovenly mistake"[59] had legs, influencing interrogation techniques on the ground for many years. Foreign policy and detention practices were also affected by these malleable memos.

Sloppy interpretive work rendered by authoritative people needs to be checked—in all senses of the word—by flexiphobes, those who have trained themselves to fear and resist rapid departures from what has been working, or it will wreak many, many years of havoc.

2. Later, Bush-era Deformations, and One Emerging Flexiphobe, Philip Zelikow

The post-9/11 chapters in the never-ending story of overly flexible responses to emergencies move forward from the relatively early Yoo-Bybee memos. Toward mid-decade, flexiphobes of a red-state stripe had begun to reassert the primacy of established codes, laws, treaties, and constitutional meanings. It was a few conservatives in Congress who tended to take the lead against the newly justified practices, reminding everybody that there were ensconced traditions worthy of respect and that these embedded habits of mind did not tolerate torture or other related practices. One of these *red-staters* was Senator John McCain who, in 2005, spearheaded the "McCain Amendment" extending as a matter of US law the Convention against Torture's prohibition on "acts of cruel, inhuman, or degrading treatment."[60] McCain and many speaking for the Army at the time[61] were patriots and "red-staters," who, as McCain put it:

> have no grief for them [the terrorists], but what we are is a nation that upholds values and standards of behavior and treatment of all people, no matter how evil or bad they are.[62]

The president signed off on the amendment, and the law itself—called the Detainee Treatment Act—went into effect in late 2005.

The Detainee Treatment Act had many loopholes, which were exacerbated, secretly, by a Justice Department interpretation that exempted, flexibly, CIA interrogation practices such as waterboarding. A man named Steven Bradbury, who had originally responded flexiphobically to the Yoo memo by exclaiming "this is insane, who wrote this?" apparently flip-flopped; as Professor Cole observes:

> For his part, Bradbury wrote three memos in 2005 and one in 2007, all of which concluded that the CIA could continue to engage in whatever coercive tactics it approved.[63]

Would there be sanity within the executive branch on a par with some of the red-stater senatorial behavior? The answer at mid-decade seemed to be "Sadly, no!" until just recently it was revealed that there *was* a flexiphobe in the tradition of Maury, Lainé, and especially Judge Kreyssig! His name, newly emerged from the obscurity of suppressed documents into the light of Freedom-of-Information-Act day, was Philip Zelikow, a former dean and professor of law at the University of Virginia, who was working in the Bush state department. He used this base, we now find out, to protest. As a twenty-first-century iteration of history's dogged "Pharisees," Zelikow bucked the trend, early in 2006, by issuing a five-page internal memorandum insisting that "several of these [interrogation] techniques, singly or in combination, should be considered 'cruel, inhuman, or degrading treatment or punishment'" and that the "techniques least likely to be sustained are the techniques described as 'coercive,' especially viewed cumulatively, such as the water board, walling, dousing, stress positions, and cramped confinement."[64]

Zelikow said later that he felt he had to get the president's attention; all he wanted to do was to make "an argument that says your interpretation of the law appears to this one fellow [me] to be unsound."[65] "It was bureaucratically and personally awkward for a state department official to challenge the department of justice on the interpretation of American constitutional law," he said, "but I had worked on constitutional law years earlier."[66]

3. Up to the Present: On Obama's Watch, or "Targeted Killing Comes to Define War on Terror"

i. "When Lawyers Evolve" to Targeted Killings

What happens when the opposite party of "Enlightened Ones" takes over in the midst of a tradition-bending process? Like most people whose politics are similar to mine, I welcomed the presence of Barack Obama in the White House. I continue to admire him deeply. But on the question of how dubious Bush-era "emergency" measures might have been tempered or eliminated on Obama's watch, relatively recent history cautioned me against optimism in that regard.[67]

There is no moral comparison between the post-9/11 practices I discuss here and the grotesque compromises of the Hitler period in Europe detailed so far in this study. Obama is a fine thinker, and he has (if only quite recently) become explicitly aware of what he calls the "compromises" to our basic values unfortunately reached after 9/11. In the perspective of some progressive thinkers that I admire greatly, liberal critics of the president's national security policies have insufficiently recognized the laudatory shifts from Bush-era attitudes rendered by Obama.[68] They may well be correct, and I believe the judgment of history will be in President Obama's favor. My interest here is less directed to history's future judgments than to its past lessons, rehearsed earlier in this book. And while there is no moral equivalency whatsoever between post 9/11 policies by any administration and history's darkest moments, I worry explicitly about the near-predictability of regrettable shifts wrought by flexible policy makers in times of perceived and virtually never-ending "emergencies."

In assessing, for example, the transition to the characteristically excellent people Obama brought in to the transition team on national security, I do think about Joseph Barthélemy, a highly distinguished law professor who in 1941 accepted Marshal Pétain's invitation to become Vichy's second minister of justice. A prewar anti-fascist and anti-antisemite, Barthélemy replaced a vicious xenophobe, Raphael Alibert. The latter's hatred of Jews helped explain the regime's early and noncoerced entry into the field of what I have called here the "anti-Talmudic" strain of anti-semitic legislation. Alibert's extreme personality wound up alienating even his own Vichy colleagues, and the Germans sensed he was as opposed to them as he was to the Jews. So a fresh light was invited down to Vichy. When Barthélemy came to power, he received hopeful congratulatory telegrams and letters from moderate French men and women who were certain he would reverse his predecessor's extreme program and restore the great traditions of egalitarian France.[69]

In fact, in his subtlety and equivocation, Barthélemy worsened Vichy's record exponentially in all areas of human rights; he toughened Alibert's laws against Jews on French soil; he established special courts that dispensed with rights of appeal and other safeguards of French criminal law; he tolerated abuses that, as a great professor of law, he would earlier have abhorred and criticized.[70]

Barthelemy's example, once assimilated, provokes caution in assuming that even right-minded people, once called to power, will proceed to follow their inclinations to safeguard sound traditions. Flexibility, as I am arguing, has become a centuries-old tactic, the only pathway that power seems to take when faced with a conflict between an existing established goodness and the challenges of an apparent "emergency." I counsel tempering the lure of the "new" with a constant recognition of the risks of flexible distortion, of too quick and too dexterous a departure from soundness.

So far, with the two exceptions that follow (drones and Guantanamo, and putting eavesdropping aside), the Obama approach inspires hope that constitutional norms and the rule of law are gradually cabining decisions on how to combat global terrorism.

President Obama is obviously a man of good will, and to many like myself also one whose "informed intuition," as I have been calling it, is usually sound. Events, however, can ride herd over fine qualities when flexibility, as so often happens, supersedes good judgment as a strategic baseline on key issues of leadership.

A case in point is the use of "targeted killings." A few weeks after the tenth anniversary of 9/11, an American-born Muslim cleric named Anwar al-Awlaki was the victim of a missile strike in Yemen.[71] Information emerged later that such targeted killings had been authorized by a team that included some of the fiercest critics of Bush-era practices; they had been brought into Obama's Office of Legal Counsel.[72] As one commentator put it:

> The secret document provided the justification for acting despite an executive order barring assassinations, a federal law against murder, protections in the Bill of Rights and various strictures of the international laws of war.... The legal analysis, in essence, concluded that Mr. Awlaki could be legally killed, if it was not feasible to capture him, because intelligence agencies said he was taking part in the war between the United States and Al Qaeda and posed a significant threat to Americans, as well as because Yemeni authorities were unable or unwilling to stop him.[73]

No wonder that conservative media underscored the irony that external critics, once inside the doors to power, often change their stripes and compromise the principles they previously propounded. The *National Review on Line* (NRO) chided "critics of the Bush administration's claims of executive authority"; in a piece relevantly headlined "When Lawyers Evolve," NRO took the opportunity to flatter its conservative readers with a form of sarcastic moral equivalency:

> Assassination by Hellfire missile being more invasive than water boarding,...the Occupy Wall Street protests will morph into "Obama lied" protests." Sooner than later, the *New York Times* and MSNBC will lead calls [that the memo writers should be] fired from their faculty positions and disbarred.[74]

The ironies apparently implicated here were furthered when, as I emphasized in an earlier chapter, Senator Rand Paul (who took some ridiculing in the liberal media for this) became the main voice, and a red-state one at that, to insist that CIA-nominee John Brennan not be confirmed until the Justice Department gave more information on drones to the Senate, which they did fairly quickly.[75]

As this book goes to press, the "debate" on drone strikes seems to have expanded to cover some Democrat voices in opposition.[76] But there is still very little to indicate that a Jacques Maury is emerging, or an Abraham Lainé, or a Judge Lothar Kreyssig, or a Philip Zelikow for that matter, to drive to the level of dogma an insistence on finding out what our government is doing.

ii. *The Gitmo Issue Is Not Going Away*

Equally as alive as the drone situation is the package of issues connected to Guantanamo that perhaps most links the red-state W. Bush policies to their variations in Obama's blue-state White House. In April 2013, a "Guantanamo hunger strike enters its third month":

The circumstances that led to the start of the hunger strike in February parallel what took place seven years earlier [and] appear to have been sparked by actions undertaken by Joint Task Force-Guantanamo to search prisoners' Korans for "contraband." These searches were in response to five suicide attempts in May 2006 and the death last September of Adnan Farhan Abdul Latif....

"They had great hope Guantanamo would be closed," [SOUTHCOM commander General John] Kelly said. "They were devastated apparently when the president backed off, at least their perception, of closing the facility.

Kelly told lawmakers, however [testifying before the House Armed Services Committee], he did believe the intention of the hunger strikers was to "turn up the heat, get it back in the media."

In that regard, the prisoners have succeeded. The hunger strike has become an international news story and a public relations nightmare for the government. It even merited a rare mention Wednesday by White House Deputy Press Secretary John Earnest, who said "The White House and the President's team is closely monitoring the hunger strikers at Guantanamo Bay.[77]

As to the "monitoring," the media greeted it subsequently with such very telling headlines as *Truthout*'s "*Déjà vu*: defense Officials Downplay Growing Guantanamo Strike with Bush-Era Talking Points."[78]

But what of this book's lesson—that intransigent responses are called for when our baseline beliefs and traditions are threatened? In the endless "war on terror," isn't this a justification for compromising the norms against limitless detention and undignified treatment of prisoners? Has this book not counseled that the overt show of inflexibility by our adversaries should assist us to become even more firmly committed to our side of the battle with them? Yet, in the Guantanamo situation, are we certain that those imprisoned there really are or ever were "our adversaries"? If troubled, should we remain silent because the government knows so much more than we do? Should we be influenced by people we tend to admire (liberal academicians entering the administration of President Obama, a leader we—or at least I, individually—admire)?

As Avishai Margalit's *Rotten Compromises* suggested,[79] the slippery slope toward questionable actions made in our name as citizens of a country begins, of course, with just such rationalizations. How much time should we spend rationalizing, when our advanced intuition keeps telling us there is something wrong? Time can be of the essence, because over-reflection and limitless researching into new facts can combine to permit bizarre new policies to gain a foothold while those opposed remain silent or add their voices to an Enlightened equivocation.

Notes

1. Sanford Levinson, *Constitutional Faith* (Princeton, NJ: Princeton University Press, 1988).

2. See, e.g., Kent Greenawalt, *Legal Interpretation: Perspectives from Other Disciplines and Private Texts* (New York: Oxford University Press, 2010); Jaroslav Pelikan, *Interpreting the Bible and the Constitution* (New Haven, CT: Yale University Press, 2004).

3. William Brennan, "The Constitution of the United States: Contemporary Ratification," reprinted in S. Levinson and S. Mailloux, *Interpreting Law and Literature* (Evanston, IL: Northwestern University Press, 1988) at pp. 17ff. See also Jack M. Balkin's comprehensive treatment of the theme in *Living Originalism* (Cambridge, MA: Harvard University Press, 2011).

4. Of course, as discussed in Chapter 3, the rich Jewish interpretive tradition embraces far more than the stiff-necked search for literalism

usually ascribed to it by the first four centuries of Christian misread-ings. Similarly, a "strict constructionist" of the Constitution may take a highly complex and ethical pathway to her sense of allegiance to the text; see, e.g., Paul Brest, "The Misconceived Quest for the Original Understanding," *Boston University Law Review* 60 (1980).

5. But see Justice Ruth Bader Ginsburg's long-standing position, reiterated in early 2013, that the abortion issue might better have been left to the political process and that *Roe* may have set back full implementation of a woman's right to choose. See *The New York Times* editorial "Justice Ginsburg's Misdirection," from April 2, 2013. Part of *Roe*'s problem, for me, was its very awkward mode, formally and stylistically, of locating the right it found, but that task was adequately if not brilliantly handled by Justice Douglas in his dazzling concurrence, which explains in a few lines why women should have rights of full autonomy over their reproductive decisions.

6. See my "Text into Theory: A Literary Approach to the Constitution," *Georgia Law Review* 20 (1986): 993, reprinted and revised in Levinson and Mailloux, *Interpreting Law and Literature,* pp. 181–93.

7. Professor Levinson himself has long since abandoned *his* faith. Sanford Levinson, *Our Undemocratic Constitution* (New York: Oxford University Press, 2006), which he elaborates in *Framed: America's 51 Constitutions and the Crisis of Governance* (New York: Oxford University Press, 2012).

8. Levinson, *Constitutional Faith*; Professor Levinson reiterates the religious analogies connected to constitutional interpretation in *Framed,* at 272ff.

9. See, e.g., Ronald Dworkin, *Taking Rights Seriously* (Cambridge, MA: Harvard University Press, 1978), pp. 14–80. See Balkin, *Living Originalism,* n. 3, at p. 350: "What motivates [Dworkin's] distinction between rules and principles is whether the norm in question is mandatory or whether it merely has weight."

10. See Chapter 5, note 4. "The nature of things," the *Bradwell* court decided, was that women belonged in the kitchen. *Bradwell v. State,* 16 Wall (83 US) 130 (1873), concurrence of Bradley, J.

11. Levinson and Mailloux, p. 262.

12. *Hans v. Louisiana,* 134 US 9 (1890).

13. Balkin, *Living Originalism,* n. 3 at p. 454; n. 39.

14. Holdsworth, *A History of the English Law* (London: 1903), vol. IX, p. 90.

15. From the pen of another recent analyst of the Eleventh Amendment, Michael Landau:

> Short and seemingly clear, the Eleventh Amendment of the United States Constitution has nonetheless been the subject of some of the Supreme Court's most convoluted and unprincipled constitutional interpretation.... Over the years, the Supreme Court—often as a function of its composition—has varied in its answers to the questions of what the language means, which suits are barred, and what relation the amendment has to other legislation. (*Fordham Intellectual Property, Media & Entertainment Law Journal* 22 [2012]: 513).

16. See, e.g., Justice Douglas in *Petty v. Tennessee-Missouri Bridge Commission*, 359 US 275 (1959), where the Court found an implied waiver of the state's immunity from suit by an out-of-stater; and *Parden v. Terminal Railroad Co.*, 377 US 184 (1963), where the Court interpreted a congressional employment-related statute to convey a right to a remedy, even against a state that would otherwise be immune under *Hans*.

17. *Plessy v. Ferguson*, 163 US 537 (1896).

18. Flexiphobic Judge Lothar Kreyssig heroically and openly bemoaned the tendency of Nazi-era judges to ignore the rules they were trained in and to determine outcomes according to the principle of what would the Fuehrer want? See Chapter 4, e.

19. 163 US 537 (1896), p. 552.

20. See, among many recitations of this *Plessy* through *Brown* story of hard, flexiphobic work, A. Leon Higgenbotham Jr., "Keeping Thurgood Marshall's Promise," *Harvard Blackletter Journal* 16 (2000).

21. We need to celebrate each federal district court judge in the South who remained true to *Brown* during the explosive years 1954–65, until the political branches finally became active in supporting the decision—Eisenhower had sent in the troops to desegregate the University of Alabama, but that was the prior high point. See, e.g., the obituary of Judge Frank M. Johnson, "Whose Rulings Helped Desegregate the South," *New York Times*, July 24, 1999, p. A12.

22. Wechsler, "Toward Neutral Principles of Constitutional Law," *Harvard Law Review* 73 (1959): 1.

23. 249 US 47 (1919).

24. 330 US 1 (1947).

25. Citing *The Federalist Papers* #37 in my "On the Use and Abuse of Nietzsche for Modern Constitutional Theory," in Levinson and Mailloux, *Interpreting Law and Literature*, 181.

26. See, e.g., Gerald Gunther, "Clear and Present Danger in the Forties: Widening Use, Rising Dissatisfaction," in Gunther, *Constitutional Law*, 12th ed. (Westbury, NY: Foundation Press, 1991), 1040 ff. Gunther has been instrumental in elaborating reasons for Holmes's much faster "dissatisfaction" with his own test; see *Constitutional Law*, p. 1019, n. 5 and Gunther's career-long scholarly work on Judge Learned Hand, who confided in Holmes his doubts about the just-decided Schenck case; see Gunther, "Learned Hand and the Origins of Modern First Amendment Doctrine: Some Fragments of History," *Stanford Law Review* 27 (1975): 719 ff. Most recently, Thomas Healy tells the story quite differently, and with unnecessary reverence for Holmes, in *The Great Dissent* (New York: Metropolitan, 2013).

27. *Abrams v. US*, 250 US 616 (1919), affirming under the clear and present danger test the conviction of political protesters under the Espionage Act of 1917 that had condemned Schenck, but this time with a dissenting opinion by Holmes.

28. *Brandenburg v. Ohio*, 395 US 444 (1969).

29. On "Face the Nation," March 31, 2013, Cardinal Timothy Dolan reiterated the widespread belief that Americans continue to be a religious people, although allowing a figure of 20% who had no religious affiliation, ascribing this to "some troubles with the church."

30. See http://www.constitution.org/tj/sep_church_state.htm for the Jeffersonian origins or the "wall of separation." While Jefferson saw a threat to the secular from religion, Roger Williams saw any commingling as a risk to religion; see his "Mr. Cotton's Letter Lately Printed, Examined, and Answered" (1644).

31. *Rosenberger v. University of Virginia*, 515 US 819 (1995), Justice O'Connor concurring.

32. Thomas, J., dissenting to a denial of certiorari in *US Highway Patrol v. American Atheists*. Justice Thomas wanted to hear the case because "the court should be deeply troubled by what its establishment clause jurisprudence has wrought." Arguably, however, he has contributed mightily to the chaos as the lone justice who would overrule *Everson's*

finding that the states—like the federal government—are bound to respect the separation of church and state. *How* that respect is to be shown is radically unclear, but at least the 1947 case did bind states and localities to adhere to federal rules restricting their sponsorship of religious displays, activities, education, and fiscal aid. Justice Thomas would leave each state and locality free to create its own approach to church/state relations.

33. *District of Columbia v. Heller*, 554 US 570 (2008).

34. A. Scalia and Bryan A. Garner, *Reading Law* (Eagan, MN: West Publishing, 2012), pp. xxviii–xxx.

35. See Chapter 4, text at note 9.

36. See some tracking of Justice Scalia's inconsistencies in Jack Balkin, *Living Originalism*, pp. 7–8; 124–25. See also a scathing critique of Scalia's brand of textualism by his fellow federal judge, Richard Posner: "Review: The Spirit Killeth but the Letter Giveth Life," *The New Republic*, September 13, 2012, p. 18.

37. See *Brief for Professors of Linguistics and English . . .* Submitted to the Supreme Court in *Heller* on January 11, 2008.

38. A well-known statement by Scalia of his own skepticism about ferreting out the intentions of legislators or Framers and ratifiers is, "Men may intend what they will, but it is only the laws they enact which bind us." Amy Guttmann, ed., *A Matter of Interpretation: Federal Courts and the Law* (Princeton, NJ: Princeton University Press, 1997), pp. 16, 17. The textualist (or plain meaning) method—at least when it does away with any form of inquiry into the intent of the text's human creators—has been widely criticized (even when used consistently, which is not what Scalia has been doing). See, e.g., Stanley Fish, "Intention Is All There Is: A Critical Analysis of Aharon Barak's Purposive Interpretation in Law," *Cardozo Law Review* 29 (2008): 1109.

39. See Chapter 2, b., 2.

40. This sobriquet, "too clever by a half," describes a subcategory of infinite malleability that seems paradoxical. Isn't the detailed parsing of a relatively clear text something that has been associated through the millennia with the "Pharisaic" reader, the "Talmudist," the "Jewish scholar"? Yet, to touch on it only in a preliminary way and in the spirit of this book—see Chapter 3, notes 7, 19, and 35—Jewish oral tradition, sophistry seems more a characteristic of other more malleable traditions, where the whole text may be commandeered without apparent restraint.

41. In Sanford Levinson, *Torture: A Collection* (New York: Oxford University Press, 2004), p. 299.

42. David K. Shipler, *The Rights of the People* (New York: Vintage, 2011). Subsequent parenthetical page references to Shipler are to this volume.

43. See Chapter 2, note 2.

44. See Chapter 2, note 11.

45. *Bowers v. Hardwick*, 478 US 186 (1986), overruled by *Lawrence v. Texas*, 539 US 558 (2003), held that states could criminalize consenting sexual activity between gays or lesbians.

46. For a discussion, complication, and seeming acceptance in some circumstances, of "torture light," see theologian Jean Bethke Elshtain's essay, in Levinson, *Torture: A Collection,* n. 41, pp. 86–88.

47. See Dershowitz advocating a "torture warrant" in Levinson, ibid., p. 259.

48. The argument "credited" with validating the ticking bomb hypothetical is Michael Walzer's "The Problem of Dirty Hands," reiterated in Levinson, *Torture: A Collection*, p. 61. An effective critique of Walzer's much-discussed equivocation is in Bob Brecher, "Torture and the Ticking Bomb," reviewed on line by C. A. J. Coady at http://ndpr.nd.edu/news/23926-torture-and-the-ticking-bomb/(2/29/09).

49. *Korematsu v. US*, 323 US 214 (1941). The case was revivified in some post-9/11 rationalizations for unusual detention policies. See a description of that in Jonathan Hafetz, "Military Detention in the 'War on Terrorism': Normalizing the Exceptional after 9/11," *Columbia Law Review Sidebar* 112 (March 2012).

50. In a prominent review of the volume by Rosa Brooks, Elaine Scarry also received praise for declining the opportunity to let the emergency overwhelm her; see Rosa Brooks, Review: "Ticking Bombs and Catastrophes," *Green Bag* 2d. 8 (2005): 311. Brooks admires many other essays in the collection, e.g., John Langbein's, which tracks the history of torture and concludes that, whatever its gratifications may have been, finding the truth is not one of them. For a fine and more recent related analysis, see Alexandra D. Lahav, "Portraits of Resistance: Lawyer Responses to Unjust Proceedings," *UCLA Law Review* 57 (2010): 725. As I wrote:

> Although the practice of torture violates all of our traditions, lawyers of impeccable credentials are starting to "pull a Vichy" on their community. Lacking the will to mount a Maury-style protest,

they seek to cabin torture within a spectrum of acceptable and unacceptable procedures and definitions. In this sense they exceed the unfortunate example of Vichy . . . [where] the legal community's eventual looseness managed to *enhance*, grotesquely, the racial laws' chances of succeeding; today, loose professionalism may in fact *create the practice*. [And] today's loose professionals have World War II and its lessons fully behind them. (Weisberg, in Levinson, *Torture*, 303–4, emphases in original)

51. Richard Posner, *Not a Suicide Pact: The Constitution in a Time of National Emergency* (New York: Oxford University Press, 2003).

52. Harold Bloom hints at what I am calling in my conclusion the restoration of sound textual traditions when he says in *Jesus and Yahweh* that the "textual slavery" suffered by the Hebrew Bible at the hands of Christian exegetes may someday end: "Yahweh may not yet have spoken his final word on this matter" (p. 37).

53. Karen J. Greenberg and Joshua L. Dratel, eds., *The Torture Papers* (New York: Cambridge University Press, 2005); subsequent parenthetical page references within this section are to this book.

54. See, e.g., David Cole, "The Sacrificial Yoo: Accounting for Torture in the OPR Report," *Journal of National Security Law & Policy* 4 (2010): 457–60.

55. See. e.g., Leopold and Kaye, "'Guidebook to False Confessions': Key Document John Yoo Used to Draft Torture Memo Released," http://truth-out.org/news/item/8278-exclusive-guidebook-to-false-confessions-key-document-john-yoo-used-to-draft-torture-memo-released (April 4, 2012).

56. OPR as cited in Cole, "The Sacrificial Yoo," note 54, p. 456.

57. Ibid.

58. Ibid., p. 457.

59. Ibid., p. 455; see also Peter Friedman, "Ruling Imagination: Law and Creativity," February 20, 2010, blogs.geniocity.com/friedman/tag/michael-mukasey.

60. The McCain Amendment was passed overwhelmingly by the Senate on October 5, 2005.

61. The Army and McCain did not totally agree, but both conservative voices tended to try to preserve existing anti-torture traditions. For a timeline of the Detainee Treatment Act, which describes McCain's and

the Army's initiatives at the time, see http://fpc.state.gov/documents/organization/76919.pdf.

62. December 15, 2005, "Pres. Bush Holds Media Availability with Senator McCain," *Washington Post.com.*

63. Cole, "The Sacrificial Yoo," note 54, p. 459.

64. Recently Unclassified Zelikow memo of February 15, 2006; see, e.g., "Memo Shows US Official Disagreed with Bush Administration's View on Torture," April 3, 2012, reported at http://www.guardian.co.uk/world/2012/apr/04/george-bush-state-department-torture/print.

65. See Zelikow interview on the Rachel Maddow show of April 21, 2009, at http://videocafe.crooksandliars.com/heather/philip-zelikow-white-house-attempted-destroy.

66. *New York Times*, April 8, 2013, p. A1.

67. The article title referenced in the preceding head, "Targeted Killing Comes to Define War on Terror," is by Scott Shane, *New York Times*, April 7, 2013, p. A1. Shane reports that 65 percent of Americans, doubtless influenced by a decade or more of flexible equivocation about all post-9/11 departures from sound practice, "approved of strikes to kill suspected terrorists." See also Chapter 2, n. 11.

68. See David Cole, "Breaking Away," *The New Republic*, Dec. 8, 2010 and "After September 11: What We Still Do Not Know!" in *New York Review of Books*, Sept. 29, 2011.

69. For the story of the transformation of power from Alibert to Barthélemy, see Weisberg, *Vichy Law*, chapter 4, "Barthélemy."

70. The whole complex story is told in Barthélemy's own memoir (he died while under arrest just after the Liberation, but his grandson edited the wartime papers), *Ministre de la Justice* (Paris: Pygmalion, 1989).

71. Awlaki was targeted and killed on September 30, 2011. He was a major operative in al Qaeda.

72. See Charlie Savage, "US Memo Made the Legal Case to Kill a Citizen Accused of Terrorism," *New York Times*, October 9, 2011, p. A11.

73. Ibid. The update of this story involves the revelation of the "white paper" justifying (or purporting to do so) the practice. "Congress to See Memo Backing Drone Attacks on Americans," *New York Times*, February 6, 2013, p. A1. The charge of "hypocrisy" leveled at the Obama

administration is less important than the charge of what this book calls "continuing flexibility" with basic sound traditions. See also Jeremy Scahill, *Dirty War: The World Is a Battlefield* (New York: Perseus, 2013).

74. Carrie Severino, "When Lawyers Evolve," *National Review Online*, October 10, 2011, http://www.nationalreview.com/bench-memos/279658/when-lawyers-evolve-carrie-severino. See also David Cole who, even in a generally favorable account of Obama's policies, regrets the secrecy of the drone program. Although Prof. Cole applauds the current greater reliance on the rule of law, including the Authorization for the Use of Military Force, he wonders whether the policy "accords with basic principles of constitutional and international law," Cole, NYRB, cited this chapter at note 68.

75. See Chapter 2, note 2.

76. *New York Times*, February 6, 2013: "Hazards of Drone Strikes Face Rare Public Scrutiny," p. A1; April 7, 2013, "A Secret Deal on Drones, Sealed in Blood," p. A1.

77. See Jason Leopold, April 1, 2013, http://www.truth-out.org/news/item/15442-defense-officials-downplay-growing-guantanamo-hunger-strike:with-bush-era-talking-points. See also, "Gitmo Is Killing Me," *New York Times*, op ed, April 15, 2013, p. A19. See, most recently, Adam Goldman and Matt Apuzzo, "After 9/11, CIA Secretly Turned Some Gitmo Prisoners into Double Agents," AP, November 26, 2013.

78. Jason Leopold, on April 9, 2013, at http://www.truth-out.org/news/item/15442-defense-officials-downplay-growing-guantanamo-hunger-strike:with-bus-era-talking-points.

79. Margalit, this volume, Chapter 2, b., 2.

Conclusion, with a Hint on "Performing Our Values"

I have argued that we need to change our baseline approach to serious issues and valued texts. When we fall back on flexibility, as we have for 2,000 years or so, we gain the good feelings that go with our own open-mindedness, but we lose our grounding. Privileged throughout these pages has been the habituated reliance on what really counts for us, the unwillingness to surrender excellent embedded values, particularly when so-called emergencies happen (all the time, or so it often seems). I call this habit of mind and response "intransigence" and those who practice it "flexiphobes."

The deck has been deliberately stacked against flexiphobes. The problem is not that they include many with whom we sharply, sometimes mortally, disagree; rather, we respond to disagreements with fundamentalists by questioning the validity of *any* strongly held positions, thus fatally avoiding the public expression of *our own* deepest beliefs and traditions, except the darling among them, which is our own ability to compromise.

Further to sustain our sense that we should always be flexible, religious incursions of several millennia ago disdained interpretive faithfulness and excoriated "Pharisees" and all those who were steadfast. The Enlightenment tradition, based on the individual capacity to reason, largely replicated in a secular context the tendency to limitless tolerance matched by multiple methods of rationalization, equivocation, and flexibility. This, I have argued, is why so many quick, harmful changes occur; only later is there a reinstatement of—or what Martin Luther King Jr. called a "return to"—the correct, prior position. It is by then far too late for those who have been hurt during the flexible interim.

Our very vocabulary undergirds and flatters the maneuverable mind and its frequent surrender to bad influences. Those who resist may gain our admiration after the fact, but in the heat they are labeled intractable, stubborn, hardnosed, dogmatic, or at best "unrealistic." Ironically, faithfulness to one's own program is so disfavored that people use words like "flexible" when they actually mean they will become *more rigid*.

Maybe upon this book's publication, some reinstating of our finer domestic traditions and of our more idealistic global policies, despite the admitted complexity of any issue, will have occurred. Otherwise, the intransigent among us continue to enlist new troops.

These strong-minded allies need to mesh uncompromising policies and values with a *finesse of performance* that helps to get the job done. Everywhere in this book, I have suggested that negotiation combines an *overt* willingness to compromise with a deep-seated unwillingness to give the most precious part of our program away! We need a bit of Lyndon B. Johnson in his dealings with the Senate, say, on civil rights, and a bit of what Herman Melville brilliantly describes, in *Billy Budd, Sailor*, as "considerate communication."[1] Adeptness in the performance of our values must be ever-present, but identifying and sticking with those values come first.

Note

1. Melville, *Billy Budd, Sailor* (written between 1886 and 1891), ed. Harrison Hayford and Merton M. Sealts (Chicago: University of Chicago Press, 1960), ch. 4.

Bibliography

Balkin, Jack. *Living Originalism*. Cambridge, MA: Harvard University Press, 2011.

Bloom, Harold. *Jesus and Yahweh*. New York: Penguin, 2005.

Carroll, James. *Constantine's Sword*. Boston: Houghton Mifflin, 2001.

Cole, David. "The Sacrificial Yoo: Accounting for Torture in the OPR Report." *Journal of National Security Law and Policy* 4 (2010): 457–60.

Drapac, Vesna. *War and Religion, Catholics in the Churches of Occupied Paris*. Washington, DC: Catholic University of America Press, 1998.

Faulkner, William. *Intruder in the Dust*. New York: Vintage, 1996; first published 1948.

Fraser, David. *The Jews of the Channel Islands and the Rule of Law*. Brighton, UK: Sussex Academic Press, 2000.

Gallwey, W. Timothy, Edd Hanzelik, and John Horton. *The Inner Game of Stress*. New York: Random House, 2009.

Glaspell, Susan. *A Jury of Her Peers*. Whitefish, MT: Kessinger Publishing, 2004; first published 1917.

Greenberg, Karen J., and Joshua L. Dratel, eds. *The Torture Papers*. New York: Cambridge University Press, 2005.

Guttmann, Amy, and Dennis F. Thompson. *The Spirit of Compromise*. Princeton, NJ: Princeton University Press, 2012.

Hertz, J. H., ed. *Pentateuch and Haftorah*, 2d ed. London: Soncino, 1960.

Hoenig, Samuel N. *The Essence of Talmudic Law*. Northvale, NJ: Aronson, 1993.

Isaiah. Hebrew text and English translation. Introduction and commentary by I. W. Slotki. London: Soncino, 1961.

Kermode, Frank. *The Genesis of Secrecy*. Cambridge, MA: Harvard University Press, 1979.

Klinghoffer, David. *Why the Jews Rejected Jesus*. New York: Doubleday, 2006.

Levine, Amy-Jill, and Marc Z. Brettler, eds. *The Jewish Annotated New Testament*. New York: Oxford University Press, 2011.

Levinson, Sanford, ed. *Torture: A Collection*. New York: Oxford University Press, 2004.

Levinson, Sanford, and Steven Mailloux, eds. *Interpreting Law and Literature*. Evanston, IL: Northwestern University Press, 1988.

Littell, Franklin. *The Crucifixion of the Jews*. New York: Harper & Row, 1975.

Margalit, Avishai. *On Compromise and Rotten Compromises*. Princeton, NJ: Princeton University Press, 2010.

Marrus, Michael, and Robert Paxton. *Vichy France and the Jews* (New York: Basic Books, 1981).

Meeks, Wayne A. *The Origins of Christian Morality*. New Haven, CT: Yale University Press, 1993.

Mnookin, Robert. *Bargaining with the Devil*. New York: Simon and Schuster, 2010.

Mueller, Ingo. *Hitler's Justice: The Courts of the Third Reich*. Cambridge, MA: Harvard University Press, 1993.

Nietzsche, Friedrich. *The Dawn of Day*. Translated by J. M. Kennedy. In *The Complete Works of Friedrich Nietzsche*, edited by Oscar Levy. New York: Russell and Russell, 1964; original work published 1881.

Pelikan, Jaroslav. *Interpreting the Bible and the Constitution*. New Haven, CT: Yale University Press, 2004.

Sanders, E. P. *Paul, the Law, and the Jewish People*. Philadelphia: Fortress, 1983.

Scarry Elaine. *Thinking in an Emergency*. Cambridge, MA: Harvard University Press, 2011.

Shakespeare, William. *Hamlet*. In *Complete Works of Shakespeare*. Edited by Hardin Craig and David Bevington. Glenview, IL: Scott, Foresman, 1973.

Shipler, David K. *The Rights of the People: How Our Search for Safety Invades Our Liberties*. New York: Vintage, 2011.

Smith, Hazel R. Knowles. *The Changing Face of the Channel Islands*. Houndmills, Basingstoke, UK: Palgrave Macmillan, 2007.

Stolleis, Michael. *The Law under the Swastika: Studies on Legal History in Nazi Germany*. Translated by Thomas Dunlap. Chicago: University of Chicago Press, 1998.

Weisberg, Richard H. *The Failure of the Word: The Protagonist as Lawyer in Modern Fiction*. New Haven, CT: Yale University Press, 1984.

Weisberg, Richard H. *Vichy Law and the Holocaust in France*. New York: New York University Press, 1996.

Weiss-Rosmarin, Trudy. *Judaism and Christianity: The Differences*. New York: Jewish Book Club, 1943.

Index

National Rifle Association, 16
Natural Law, flexible risks of,
  106, 110n27
  and Carl Schmitt, 106
  and Justice Bradley, 118
Nietzsche, Friedrich, 56, 58

Obama, Barack, x, 29, 30, 35, 36,
  156, 158, 161
O'Connor, Justice Sandra
  Day, 141
Origen. *See* allegory
Osler, William, 6, 24n1, 25n4

Paul, Rand, 30, 53n2, 159.
  See also filibuster
Pelikan, Jaroslav, 60, 61, 79n7
Pétain, Marshal Philippe, 86, 94.
  See also Catholic Church
  inquiry to; France, Vichy
Pharisees, 10–12,
Posner, Judge Richard A.
  and flexiphobic defense of
  post-9/11 policies, 150
Postmodernism, 26n12, 54n8
Post-9/11 policies, 4, 8, 20, 30,
  36, 44–45, 50, 146–66
  and eavesdropping, 9, 36, 146,
  147, 150
  and Guantanamo, 50, 147,
  159–61
  and targeted killings, 147, 158
  and torture, 9, 30, 36, 45, 50,
  53n2, 54n11, 127, 148,
  151–53
  and unlimited detention, 9,
  30, 147
  See also emergency
Protestants, 105, 126

and Le Chambon-sur-Lignon,
  105–6
and Lutheranism of Lothar
  Kreyssig, 106

Rabin, Yitzhak, 26n14
Red-Staters vs. Blue-Staters, x,
  18, 28–31, 35, 44, 45, 53n1,
  126, 147
  and "red-baiting," 29
Rushdie, Salman, 22, 48
Russell, Bertrand, 52

Saint John
  and "B–plot" lacerating Jewish
  intransigence, 64–78
  and limitless interpretive
  flexibility, 10–12
  See also Christianity, early
  writings
Saint Paul
  and enduring influence on
  secular policy, xii, 126,
  131, 137
  and precedent of interpretive
  flexibility for WWII Catholic
  Church, 93–99
  See also Christianity, early
  writings
Scalia, Justice Antonin, 115,
  142–46
  and flexibly betraying his
  own guidelines, 142–43,
  165n38
Scarry, Elaine, 6, 23, 51, 114, 149
  and "rigidity," 6, 149
Schmitt, Carl, 54n12, 106,
  110n27. *See also* Natural
  Law, flexible risks of